RAYMOND ROUSSEL

RAYMOND ROUSSEL

A Critical Study

By Rayner Heppenstall

UNIVERSITY OF CALIFORNIA PRESS

BERKELEY AND LOS ANGELES · 1967

University of California Press
Berkeley and Los Angeles,
California

Printed in Great Britain

CONTENTS

PREFATORY NOTE

More than thirty years after his death, four works by Raymond Roussel *are* to appear in English translation, one of them on the same day as the present volume. Roussel is almost totally unknown in the English-speaking world. It seemed reasonable to accompany the first translation with a little book on the man himself and his other work and on some aspects of the translated work which do not appear on the surface and which he thought worth explaining, posthumously.

For his working methods were very strange indeed, and, in forming his own personal judgment upon an unfamiliar writer, the critic, if not the unprofessional reader, may feel that he needs some information about them. This is a critical guide only in that sense. Its purpose is documentary, not judicial.

In writing it, I contracted three debts, to Barbara Bray, J. B. Brunius and Michel Butor. Mrs. Bray got me things found with difficulty in Paris bookshops. MM. Brunius and Butor lent me otherwise unavailable Rousseliana. I am grateful to them, and merely to set their names down gives me pleasure. Indebtedness of a less personal order will, I hope, appear sufficiently in my text, together with such bibliographical aids as I thought it best to offer without a parade of scholarly apparatus.

R.H.

I

A LIFE

Rᴀʏᴍᴏɴᴅ ʀᴏᴜssᴇʟ was born on January 20th, 1877, in Paris, at 25 Boulevard Malesherbes, towards the Place de la Madeleine end. His father was a stockbroker who made a very great fortune and died early. Raymond and his sister Germaine were much of an age, but their brother, Georges, was much older. Raymond Roussel describes his childhood with Germaine as a blissfully happy one, and the two were always to remain devoted to each other.

Their mother appears to have been a woman of rare energy and idiosyncratic behaviour. Roger Vitrac, the *surréaliste* playwright, puts on record two stories that were later current about her. According to one of these, after her dinner parties, as soon as the guests had moved to the drawing-room, a beautiful woman in black, a book in her hand, descended the monumental staircase, seated herself and, opening the book, proceeded to read aloud from *The Three Musketeers* into the small hours. According to the second story, Mme. Roussel, in the winter of 1922–3, bought a yacht and had it sailed to India. As they first approached harbour, she called for a telescope and placed it to her eye. 'So that is India!' she said. 'Captain, we are returning to France!' Vitrac says that he recounted these stories to Roussel in 1924 and that Roussel did not dispute their veracity. The second of them must, however, be wrong at least as to date, since Mme. Roussel died before the outbreak of the Great War.

More reliably, Michel Leiris, whose father, Eugène Leiris, was Raymond Roussel's financial adviser and friend, informs us that Mme. Roussel went much to the Opéra and kept open house to musicians and singers. She collected eighteenth-century paintings and, when at her villa in Biarritz, kept up neighbourly relations with the family of the successful playwrights, Edmond and Maurice Rostand, father and son. Her elder son, Georges, took up sculpture.

At the age of thirteen, Raymond (this he tells us himself) left school and went to the Conservatoire, where he took up the piano and came second in examinations. At sixteen, he tried writing songs to words of his own, but soon decided that he lacked any serious gift for musical composition. He then gave himself up to writing verse.

The earliest poem extant is *Mon Âme*, a work of 544 octosyllabic lines in pairs of four-line stanzas rhymed *a b a b, a b a b*, the only substantial piece of verse Raymond Roussel was ever to compose in anything but alexandrine couplets. He then started work on *La Doublure*, a verse novel of almost six thousand lines.

His state of creative ecstasy as he worked on *La Doublure* is described for us both by Roussel and by Pierre Janet, for long the best known of French psychologists, to whom Roussel later (it is uncertain how much later) went as a patient. In his own written account, Roussel merely speaks of a sensation of universal glory (the French word *'gloire'* more closely unites the senses of our 'glory' and 'fame' and is also more commonly used than our 'glory' for haloes, aureoles, openings in the sky and such in the visual arts, as well as for the 'fixed sun' in pyrotechnics) which he experienced during a period of some months (Janet specifies five or six months) when he was nineteen. Janet, however, quotes his patient's words extensively.

It appears that the young man worked with curtains closed, because what he wrote gave off an effulgence.

I was afraid of some tiny gap letting out the rays of light which my pen gave off. I wanted to tear down the whole screen at once and illuminate the world. If I'd left those papers just lying about, the rays would have reached China, and a bewildered mob would have fallen upon the house.

2

Roussel 'knew' (and I must apologise for those inverted commas, since it is no part of the purpose of this little book to argue that he was mistaken) that he was the equal of Dante and Shakespeare. He felt what Victor Hugo felt at seventy, what Napoleon felt in 1811, what Tannhäuser dreamed in the Venusberg. The fame (the glory, the sense of glory) were not something to be created later. They existed already. The condition was one of unutterable bliss.

The work went on day and night. Roussel could hardly bear to interrupt it for a moment to go and eat a little. He did not keep still all the time, but sometimes paced about and then wrote more (such prowling is no doubt familiar to most writers). At other times, he remained motionless for hours, pen in hand, lost in his dream.

A volume of more than three hundred pages, *La Doublure* appeared on June 10th, 1897. When, he later told Janet, Raymond Roussel emerged into the street and found that nobody turned round to look at him in awe, his sense of glory turned to melancholy, and he became convinced that men were universally engaged in denigrating each other. Little notice was taken of the book. Roussel's prostration at its lack of immediate success was such that, as he tells us himself, he broke out in a rash all over his body, at first thought to be measles.

A consolatory note which reached Roussel was from Marcel Proust, to whom a copy of *La Doublure* had been sent. The two were acquainted, though it is uncertain to what extent. Proust was then twenty-six and the author only of *Les Plaisirs et les Jours*. What he specifically detected in the young poet were qualities of depth and stamina. He may also have been interested in the sea-side setting and the tomboy who fled.

A month after the publication of *La Doublure*, *Mon Âme* appeared in the Sunday *Gaulois*. During the next three years, Raymond Roussel experimented in prose and began to feel that he had found his way. In 1901, his elder brother, Georges, died. Raymond did not publish, at that time, any of his early stories in prose. In 1904, he published a second volume of verse, *La Vue*. This consisted of three poems of substantial length, *La Vue* itself, *Le Concert* and *La Source*, the three closely allied in conception, making effectively a great deal out of nothing, poems, one might say, of pure extrapolation.

The next few stories were printed, always in *Le Gaulois du Dimanche*. All this casting-about or, as he calls it, prospecting ('*de la prospection*') yet left Roussel deeply unsatisfied. In torment, he tells us, he would roll about on the floor, raging against his failure to experience those sensations of true art to which he aspired. It was not until about 1907, when he was thirty, that he hit upon verbal procedures and a method of composition which satisfied him. It is for these, only posthumously revealed, that he is best-known, even in France, today. It is inevitable that a first attempt to introduce Raymond Roussel to British and American readers must be largely preoccupied with them. They may or may not importantly constitute their originator's lasting interest. For the moment, let us attempt to proceed with the story of his life.

Two photographs show him at Dieppe in 1904. At some time before this he must have performed his military service at Amiens where, he tells us, he called on Jules Verne, who was the object of his veneration (and who died in 1905). Germaine Roussel married into the Ney family, becoming Duchess of Elchingen and later Princess of Moscow. None of the authorities gives a date for this, but, if Michel Ney was the first or only child of the marriage and was born within a reasonable interval after it, then it must have taken place by 1906. At any rate, for a great part of his life, Raymond Roussel was connected with all the families of the First Empire aristocracy, since Murats and Bonapartes were also involved. The Elchingens took up their residence in Neuilly, just to the west of Paris and bordering on the Bois de Boulogne, and for many years Roussel resided with them, though presumably not before the death of his mother.

He became a crack pistol shot, winning no fewer than forty-five medals, one of them (gold) in 1909, the year before the appearance of *Impressions d'Afrique*, the more substantial of his two great works of narrative prose. It was Edmond Rostand (author of the wildly successful *Cyrano de Bergerac* and, it may be remembered, a neighbour in Biarritz) who put it into Roussel's head to make a play out of the book, and this he promptly did. In 1911–2, he mounted a first and a revised dramatic version at his own expense in Paris and subsequently sent the revised version out on tour, not only in the provinces but abroad. The performances were noisily unsuccessful, and Roussel was described as a madman.

At about this time, according to Michel Leiris, Roussel travelled to India with his mother, the occasion perhaps of the Vitrac story. M. Leiris tells us that Mme. Roussel, troubled by the idea that she might die on the voyage, took her coffin with her. Roussel's own main preoccupation was apparently the Southern Cross, about whose appearance he constantly interrogated the crew while they were still in more northerly latitudes.

Mme. Roussel must in fact have died not long after her return to France. Her son, it appears, had a pane of glass let into the coffin, so that he would go on being able to see her face up to the very last moment, even after the lid had been screwed down. At the time, he was writing *Locus Solus*, in which brief and hallucinatory resurrection of dead people kept on ice plays an important part.

The most widely reproduced photograph of Raymond Roussel (until 1964, the only one) dates back to 1896 and was taken in Milan. It shows a young Frenchman, smartly and semi-formally dressed in short black jacket, well-creased sponge-bag trousers, stiff collar and cuffs, a broad black bow-tie presenting a surface about six inches by three. He looks clean, fastidious and, though not robust, yet perfectly virile, his colouring moderately dark, the eyes normally well-spaced and a bit deep-set, their expression conventionally aggressive. The hair, sufficiently lustrous, is parted on the left side and brushed or combed back in a fashion which must at the time have seemed very modern. For the period, the moustache also is closely trimmed, though it grows full. Any infantilism of temperament was clearly not physiological in origin. From other evidence, Raymond Roussel appears to have been a little below average height.

A name which occurs frequently in the accounts of Roussel's later years is that of Charlotte Dufrène. M. Leiris, who seems likely to remain forever our main source of biographical information about Roussel, owes much of his detail to her, though he does not tell us how she came into Roussel's life or that of his own family. From her, M. Leiris understands, among much else, that, at a time merely ascribed to 'before the war', Roussel's fastidiousness about his clothes was extreme. He would not, it seems, wear anything which had been washed even once. He never wore a collar more than once, so that, since he presumably changed often into evening clothes, he must have bought and thrown out some five hundred collars a year. He never wore a shirt or a tie more than three times or went on wearing a suit or an overcoat or a pair of braces more than a fortnight. With some variation of detail, Vitrac sets out facts of this kind as part of the legend current ten years later. Roussel must have kept dozens of servants and their friends in cast-off clothes during the immediate pre-war years.

Locus Solus appeared in 1914. Apparently in the ranks and as a driver, Raymond Roussel served in the war. Vitrac states that he questioned Roussel on the matter and quotes him as saying that he was in action and under fire at Châlons, presumably during the second (1918) and not the first battle of the Marne, since his class (he was then thirty-seven) can hardly have been called up in time for active service in 1914. In a recorded interview, apparently made in 1964 at the Jockey Club by two young men from the *Nouveaux Cahiers de Jeunesse* of Bordeaux, Michel Ney, Roussel's nephew and sole heir, describes his uncle as having been a shirker at Châlons-sur-Marne, though it must be remembered that M. Ney was then only twelve or thirteen and though his account conflicts oddly with the Dufrène-Leiris version on a number of later points. Vitrac merely reports Roussel as saying that a bombardment was a very strange thing and as reflecting on the happy coincidence that Rheims, the most bombarded city of all, should have had the biggest cellars in the world.

Though it was not completed until 1928, the elaborate *Nouvelles Impressions d'Afrique*, which, unlike the *Impressions*, is in verse, was begun in 1915. In 1918 appeared a *Pages Choisies* which contains approximately half each of *Impressions d'Afrique* and *Locus Solus*.

In 1920–1, Roussel travelled round the world in rather more than eighty days, by way of India, Australia and New Zealand, the Pacific islands, China, Japan and America. Vitrac quotes a story to the effect that, from India, Roussel sent to a woman friend, who had asked for something rare, an electric fire. After Jules Verne and Victor Hugo, 'Pierre Loti' was Roussel's favourite writer, and in Tahiti, where he stayed for some time, he tells us that he met the originals of some of the characters in *Le Mariage de Loti*, first published forty years before and describing a period eight years earlier still. Raymond Roussel travelled very widely indeed. He already knew most of Europe, as well as Egypt and North Africa. He was later to visit Constantinople, Asia Minor and Persia. He insists that, from all his travels, he drew nothing whatever for his books, that imagination was all. He did not, he told Janet, wish to write of anything 'real'. While crossing the Pacific, he stayed in his cabin, in order that, once in Tahiti, he might feel free not to work his customary three hours a day. In Peking, after a quick drive round the town, he stayed in his hotel to catch up on arrears in his writing. The title *Impressions d'Afrique* suggests a travel book, but of course it is nothing of the kind, though it is set in an imaginary Africa, a part of Africa which Roussel had not then visited or was ever to visit. Travelling itself pleased him and the means of travel. In Melbourne, he was enchanted by the plenitude of hansom cabs, as well as by the oysters and kangaroo soup.

The stage version of *Impressions d'Afrique* had been Roussel's own. That of *Locus Solus* was done to order by Pierre Frondaie, a popular playwright and novelist. It was put on luxuriously at the Antoine on December 7th, 1922. The performance was greeted with tumultuous hostility, though there was some *avant-garde* applause. After the performance, a group of young *surréalistes* forced their way backstage to express their admiration and support, and Vitrac's principal impression of Roussel was of his courteous manner and his magnificent teeth. The police closed the theatre for two days, and cuts were made before the second performance. Performances then continued for a fortnight.

Michel Leiris wrote to his late father's friend and received in reply a note, dated December 16th, which said:

Thank you, my dear Michel, for your curious and interesting letter.

I see that, like myself, you prefer the realm of Conception to that of Reality.

The interest you so kindly show in my work is to me a proof that in you I may rediscover the affection so prodigally bestowed on me by your father, and I am deeply touched.

Yours with all my heart.

What Raymond Roussel found '*curieux*' in the young Leiris's letter may have had something to do with the fact that, in his early years, M. Leiris himself was much caught up with the *surréalistes*, whose views would be quite incomprehensible to the older man. As M. Leiris himself was later to make abundantly clear, the *surréalistes'* interest in Roussel was never reciprocated. Roussel indeed never paid much attention to the *avant-garde* art or literature of his time. His taste in music, too, tended towards the currently popular. He liked Massenet, Gounod, Wagner and Reynaldo Hahn, among composers whose names we may all be expected to know, but equally admired composers of whom few of us will have heard, Paul Delmet, Xavier Privas, Théodore Botrel and Augusta Holmes. He sang their songs to his own pianoforte accompaniment at the house of Eugène Leiris, as Michel Leiris remembers from his childhood. He also did imitations of opera singers and other performers of the time and was later to write sadly that this was the only field in which he had ever enjoyed the least success.

The stage presentation of *Locus Solus* made, in a way, its mark. It was parodied in numerous revues, one of which, entitled *Cocus Solus*, ran for more than a hundred performances. It would be interesting to know when Roussel first had recourse to Dr. Janet, whom he describes as having looked after him '*pendant de longues années*'. This suggests an earlier date than 1922–3, but M. Leiris is confident that we cannot go back as far as the crisis at nineteen, though Janet was then already directing the La Salpêtrière clinic (as well as teaching philosophy both at the Lycée Condorcet and at Louis-le-Grand). Certainly, Janet describes the crisis at nineteen, but this is in Roussel's own words. Michel Ney understood that his uncle had been in a clinic at an early period. However, when Janet wrote his account of Roussel's case-history (under the name of 'Martial', after Martial Canterel, who is the central figure in *Locus Solus*), he described him as a man then of forty-five, which gives us 1922-3.[1] Nothing in what Janet says fixes the moment or the occasion exactly or, indeed, indicates that at the time there was any complete break-down. This suggests that Roussel had consulted Janet in a worse state earlier, but went to him again, in some distress and agitation, after the dreadful failure of *Locus Solus* and the public insults which ensued.

Janet describes Roussel at forty-five as living alone, but writing hard and taking joy in his work, though finding it effortful. 'I bleed,' he is reported as saying, 'over each phrase.' The work of the moment appears to have been in verse, which can only mean that Roussel had gone back momentarily to the unfinished *Nouvelles Impressions*. His faith in the destiny which awaited him was still absolute.

It may take a long time, but my fame will outshine that of Victor Hugo or Napoleon. Wagner died twenty-five years too soon to know his day of glory, I hope to live long enough to see mine. . . . There lies within me a latent glory of immense force, like that of a shell which has yet to burst. . . . The light of this glory will fall upon all my works without exception, it will illuminate every action of my life; people will avidly dig up information about my childhood and marvel at the way I played prisoner's base. . . . Some people are predestined! Then, as the poet says, one feels the brand on one's brow.[2] . . . The star one bears resplendent. . . . I shall never forget it.

[1] The first volume of *De l'Angoisse à l'Extase* appeared in 1926. It appears to be one of the few works by Janet which have never been translated into English, though it is known among students of psychology for the case to which it is largely devoted, that of 'Madeleine', a patient at La Salpêtrière, who was subject to religious delusions and who, during states of trance, produced Crucifixion stigmata on her feet. The book contains photographs of these stigmata.

[2] *Et voilà qu'on se sent une brûlure au front.* . . . This is an unmistakable alexandrine. I do not know its source, but anybody bent on tracking it down might begin worse than by working his way slowly through the voluminous works in verse, including the plays, of Victor Hugo. Tracing the line may,

I do not myself find Janet's comments helpful. He is too firmly committed to the view that true ecstasy, with its immobility and complete detachment, its life and its happiness totally outside human experience, must inevitably take a religious form, leading to divine life, to a life in God, a life as God. Janet, of course, was never to be convinced that his patient's writings had any great merit. '*Ce n'était qu'un pauvre petit malade!*' was his comment to Michel Leiris when the latter went to see him after Roussel's death.

As to the brand on the brow, the star one bears resplendent, Roussel's next work was to be a play, *L'Étoile au Front*, which concludes with a passage on the star-marked, predestinate elect, a passage quite unrelated to the rest of the play. This was put on at the Vaudeville in early May, 1924. The uproar was such that during a scene in the third act the curtain had to be lowered. This time, the *surréaliste* and other *avant-garde* supporters appear to have organised themselves somewhat. During the second act, somebody called out to those who were applauding: '*Hardi la claque!*' Robert Desnos wittily called back: '*Oui, nous sommes la claque, et vous êtes la joue!*'—the word '*claque*' meaning equally hired applauders or a slap, here on the cheek, while, as Roussel, who himself tells this story, points out, by the kind of inversion of consonants we know as a Spoonerism and regard as accidental foolishness but which to the French is a type of intentional joke, a *contrepet*, the objector could have been thought '*jaloux*'. At the close of a later performance, a gang of students waited outside the theatre to barrack Roussel, but he evaded them. There ensued a hideous controversy in the newspapers, in which leading actors and actresses were accused of dishonouring their profession by appearing in so bad a play because they were paid exceptional fees.

In 1926, Roger Vitrac was accorded an interview by Roussel, about which, however, he did not write until two years later.

indeed, be like looking for a needle in a haystack, but it will almost certainly be child's play compared with the task of establishing any conclusions about Roussel's style at prisoner's base or any more information about his childhood than has already been offered to the reader of this book.

Roussel's second play, *La Poussière de Soleils*, had by then been (in February) mounted at the Porte-Saint-Martin, with less disturbance than on the previous theatrical occasions, though it got a bad press.

A *roulotte*, caravan or house on wheels, which Roussel had had built to his own specifications, had created something of a legend. There was, for instance, an illustrated article on it in *La Revue du Touring Club de France*. It was a luxurious vehicle, with bedroom, a dining room which could be converted into a studio, a bathroom with all the conveniences and a room for the chauffeur. It travelled twice round Europe.

Vitrac reports its owner as saying:

'It is very agreeable, you stop where you want, you set off again when you want, a real land-yacht. And you're alone.'

'Alone?' said Vitrac. 'But, surely, people. . . .'

'Yes, that's true, but you can avoid the villages. Mussolini, whom I went to see in Rome, said the same thing to me. I told him that he, at any rate, had no need of a vehicle like that to attract crowds. The Pope, too, wanted to see my car. But as he can't leave the Vatican, and as, from reasons of propriety—I wonder why?—my caravan couldn't be driven in, he sent someone out to me—a Nuncio, who went away filled with admiration.'

From Vitrac's account of his visit, it would appear that, by 1926, Roussel was already accustomed to receive visitors at Charlotte Dufrène's apartment in the Rue Pierre-Charron, a practice which M. Leiris's account might have led us to think Roussel only adopted later (perhaps because not until later, when he was living in a disreputable hotel, did he take to receiving even old friends at Mme. Dufrène's). At any rate, although Roussel was apparently still resident with the Elchingens at Neuilly, Vitrac was received at '*l'appartement d'une femme*', and it was clearly in a turning off the Champs-Élysées, as the Rue Pierre-Charron is. This little street is nowadays best known to men of letters as that in which stands the *maison internationale* of the P.E.N. Club, flanked on one side by a night club called Le Sexy and facing The Chickens Self, a restaurant no doubt specialising in barbecued chicken and operated on self-service principles.

In 1927, Roussel travelled to Persia and countries adjacent. Baghdad reminded him merely of an operetta by Lecocq. In 1928, he finished the *Nouvelles Impressions* and served as foreman on a jury, his sister that year becoming also Princess of Moscow, by reason of someone's demise. In 1931, his nephew, Michel Ney, also married into a family of First Empire nobility which further included Ferdinand de Lesseps, builder of the Suez Canal, among its forebears. In the winter of 1931–2, Roussel took up chess and, after three and a half months' play, devised a formula for the difficult mate with knight and bishop to which, in the international chess monthly, *L'Échiquier*, no less a person than Tartakower devoted no fewer than three articles. This may not have been wholly disinterested. M. Leiris has told us that Roussel paid his chess-instructor's debts, without saying who the instructor was. I am assured by Harry Golombek, who knew him, that Tartakower was a compulsive gambler.

These three articles were to be included in the posthumous volume, *Comment J'Ai Écrit Certains de mes Livres*, which Roussel was then engaged in putting together. So were the pages on 'Martial' from Pierre Janet's *De l'Angoisse à l'Extase*. Apart from the introductory essay, the book's principal contents were to be a group of seventeen early stories, five other stories and poems, also early, and six (thirty had been originally planned) *Documents Pour Servir de Canevas*, the skeleton of a projected work. The book was to contain, as frontispiece, the Milan photograph of Raymond Roussel at nineteen, but in the result it never did. The bulk of the volume was put into the hands of Lemerre's master printer, Eugène Vallée, who had set all Roussel's books up, on April 16th, 1932. The *Nouvelles Impressions* came out that year, swelled out with illustrations commissioned through a detective agency and including also the early poem, *Mon Âme*, now entitled *L'Âme de Victor Hugo*. *Comment J'Ai* was to carry a dedication to Charlotte Dufrène and not to appear until after its author's death.

From chess, Roussel turned first to hard drinking and then to drugging himself with barbiturates. According to M. Leiris, some form of homosexual practice had always been his *goût exclusif*, and he moved into a Montmartre hotel frequented by homosexuals and drug-addicts. In the second half of 1932, M. Leiris himself, a professional anthropologist among other things, was on an anthropological expedition, partly financed by Roussel, in tropical Africa. He states that, on Christmas Eve, Roussel went to midnight mass at Notre Dame de Lorette. Nowhere, it may be said, in Roussel's work or in what has been recorded of his life is there any suggestion of Christian belief, though no doubt he had been brought up to normal French Catholic religious practices.

Returning to Paris at the beginning of 1933, M. Leiris called on Roussel at Mme. Dufrène's. Roussel had shaved off his moustache, was still elegantly dressed in subfusc style, still handsome but a bit heavy, his voice seeming to come from a distance. On life he smilingly reflected: '*Ça passe de plus en plus vite!*' Asked if he was writing, he said: '*C'est tellement difficile!*' In a characteristic way, he detained M. Leiris at the door. On May 30th, he went round to Lemerre's and drew up, in the form of four separate notes, his final instructions to the printer. Then, with Mme. Dufrène, whom at the time he referred to as his housekeeper (his '*gouvernante*'), he set out for Sicily.

In Palermo, they installed themselves at the Grande Albergo e delle Palme, where Wagner had written much of *Parsifal*, their adjacent rooms, Nos. 226 (Roussel's) and 227 (Mme. Dufrène's) being on the second floor at the corner of the Via Mariano Stabile[1] and the Via Riccardo Wagner, the quietest part, M. Leiris assures us, of the hotel.

His day-time use of that group of drugs we nowadays think of only as the main constituent of sleeping-pills induced in Roussel (now aged fifty-six) a distinct euphoria. The barbiturates are not commonly regarded as drugs of addiction, but, deprived for a day, Roussel cried out that his arms and legs could be cut off so long as he was given his drug. In the introductory essay which was to give

[1] Presumably named, quite early in his career, after the singer, no doubt a local hero, who was still going strong in the late 'Forties, when he sang Dr. Malaparte with great verve in an admirable *Don Pasquale* at the Cambridge Theatre in London.

its title to the posthumous volume, *Comment J'Ai Écrit Certains de mes Livres*, the expectations he had expressed to Janet ten years before had already been scaled down to the modest hope that he might enjoy '*un peu d'épanouissement posthume à l'endroit de mes livres*', but now his sense of failure was complete, and he said that he had never known a moment's happiness since childhood.

Formerly, Raymond Roussel had always been worried by any thought of pain. He had begged Mme Dufrène not so much as to mention her own nervousness before a visit to the dentist, let alone her fear of snakes, in case she infected him with her fears. At the same time, there had also been an interest in pain. M. Leiris's mother had told him that, while she was expecting her second child, Roussel had questioned her on the pains of childbirth, a strange thing, as M. Leiris says, for a man to do in those days with a woman still quite young. He could not understand her willingness to go through it again after a first experience of the horror, using the word '*récidiver*', which in French, as in terms derived in English from the same root, usually means to relapse into crime. Similarly, Roussel had formerly been much afraid of death, though, again, interested in it, as the anecdote of the pane of glass in his mother's coffin sufficiently indicates. Under the partial sedation, Mme. Dufrène was to tell M. Leiris, he now exhibited a taste for death.

But I directly translate from M. Leiris's 1954 article in *Critique*.

One morning. about seven o'clock, he was found bleeding in his bath; he had opened his veins with his razor and was laughing wildly, saying: 'How easy it is to open your veins. . . . It's nothing at all'. Afterwards, when he was no longer under the influence of drugs, he wondered how he could have done that.

A few days after their arrival in Palermo, he had asked Mme. Charlotte Dufrène to return to Paris to dismiss his servants (always generously paid) and also formulated the wish that she should give up her flat, wanting to be rid of everything which remained in Paris, his intention being to travel and not to go back there for a long time.

He was at that time so weak that he could hardly raise a glass and almost had to be fed. He slept on a mattress laid on the floor, afraid of falling out of bed when drugged. The reason he gave for not wanting to eat was that eating disturbed his 'serenity'.

One day, he got Mme. Charlotte Dufrène to write to his personal manservant: he wanted box No. *** sending and said that it contained a revolver which he wanted because, being a foreigner, he would not (he thought) be able to buy one in Palermo. He told his friend that, unfortunately, he would never have the courage to press the trigger, so perhaps she could do it for him. As she repelled the idea, he tried to make her change her mind by getting out his cheque-book and asking her how much she wanted; at each refusal, he proposed a larger sum. In the end, the letter was never sent.

At Mme. Charlotte Dufrène's instance, Roussel finally decided to go to Kreuzlingen, in Switzerland, for a disintoxication cure. On the morning of July 13th, he sent off telegrams to this effect. In the evening, he told his companion she could sleep undisturbed, for that day he felt well and had not taken too many pills. For several days the connecting door had been shut at night, whereas formerly it had remained open.

The morning of the 14th, Mm. Dufrène, hearing no sound, knocked at this door between the two rooms. Receiving no reply, she called a waiter. He entered by the corridor door, which had not been locked. Mme. Dufrène and the waiter saw Roussel lying on his mattress, which he had pushed or dragged up against the connecting door (a superhuman effort for him, in view of his state of weakness). His face was calm, rested and turned towards the door.

To bring the body back from Palermo, it had to be embalmed.

In the taped interview mentioned earlier, Roussel's nephew, Michel Ney, duke of Elchingen, largely disputes this account. Indeed, he seems to cast doubt upon the very existence of Mme. Dufrène. Inevitably, his family must have received an official communication from the mayoralty in Palermo, and it is his contention that his uncle committed suicide by opening his veins in the bath. He further states that there was no effective inheritance, since Roussel died penniless. He states, moreover, that his uncle's remains lie in the family vault at Neuilly, whereas there appears to be no doubt that they repose in the cemetery of Père-Lachaise. All this is a little confusing. For my own part, I can only state that M. Leiris strikes me as a totally creditable witness, which is as well, since it is to him that we owe almost all that we know about the man Roussel.

Jean Cocteau, who had become acquainted with Raymond Roussel during his last years and had even been given some inkling of the verbal procedures which underlie his work, wrote a glowing obituary notice of him in the *Nouvelle Revue Française* and a shorter one in the *Nouvelles Littéraires*. *Comment J'Ai Écrit Certains de mes Livres* duly appeared in 1935, its title-piece having previously appeared in the *NRF* with a preface by Michel Leiris. Thereafter, all Roussel's works effectively went out of print for thirty years. Not all of them were strictly unobtainable. As late as 1962, for instance, a single Paris bookshop was able to turn up, in mint condition and at no exaggerated price, copies of the original Lemerre edition of the two plays, of the *Nouvelles Impressions*, of *Comment J'Ai* and of the *Pages Choisies* of 1918, though not of *Impressions d'Afrique* or *Locus Solus* or the earlier poems.

During most of the intervening period, not even the *surréalistes* showed much public interest in Roussel. The mood of the time had changed. André Gide, one of Roussel's early supporters, had reported on colonial oppression in the Congo and arranged to visit Russia. Hitler was in power, the Japanese in China. The Italians were about to invade Abyssinia, and within a year of the publication of *Comment J'Ai* the Spanish civil war had begun. Writers were turning political, none more so than the *surréalistes*. Aragon was already a Communist. Perhaps *Comment J'Ai* had itself produced disillusionment among Roussel's admirers. What had appeared spontaneous was now seen to have been contrived.

The first signs of reawaking interest were in 1950, when a book by Marcel Jean and Arpad Nezei, *Genèse de la Pensée Moderne*, devoted three of its chapters to Roussel, presenting him as the culmination of a tradition deeply tinged with occultism, a view subsequently adopted by the *surréaliste* leader, André Breton (it is a view, I may say, for which there exists no evidence whatever). In the same year, the young Michel Butor wrote an essay on Roussel which is reprinted in his volume *Répertoire*, and in his *Anthologie de l'Humour Noir* Breton preceded some brief notes by Jean Ferry with four pages of his own and a reproduction of the Milan photograph of Roussel at nineteen.

This anthology had been meant to include some of Roussel's own work, but, it was stated, permission had been arbitrarily refused by the publisher. It appears that Lemerre blamed 'the family' (*i.e.*, M. Ney-Elchingen) who later blamed Lemerre. At any rate, it had by now transpired that the publication rights in Roussel were tricky, as they were to remain for some fourteen years more.

The opening chapter of even a small and tentative book like this is not the position in which bibliographical notes are commonly found, but the Roussel bibliography, itself small, contains an element of drama and somehow belongs, essentially if posthumously, to the life-story of Raymond Roussel. And here it may be said that, during the early years, '*les Anglo-Saxons*' do not show up badly, since a translation by Édouard Roditi of the opening sections of *Impressions d'Afrique* appeared in the American magazine *View* during Hitler's war, as, presumably, they could not have done had not the condition of war itself suspended the usual copyright arrangements. Since then, it is true, the only Anglo-Saxon contributions to the study of Roussel which I have been able to discover were my own and those of a young American-about-Paris, John Ashbery.

In France, there further appeared in the 'Fifties an admirable essay in two parts by Pierre Schneider in the *Cahiers du Sud* (1951), a whole book, *Une Étude sur Raymond Roussel*, by Jean Ferry (1953) with a preface by Breton subsequently reprinted in his own volume *La Clé des Champs*, and the superb article in *Critique* for October 1954 by Michel Leiris, who had betweenwhiles continued to write on, and lecture about, his father's old friend elsewhere. I suggest, nevertheless, that interest in Raymond Roussel among the French young or any other category of buyers of books rose to no considerable height until the deservedly fashionable Alain Robbe-Grillet stated, in a casual aside, that Roussel had been a main influence upon his own work.

In 1963, Messrs. Gallimard put out a reprint of *Locus Solus*, together with a small book on Roussel by Michel Foucault. *Locus Solus* was meant to be the first of a comprehensive series of reprints. It has not been disclosed on precisely what legal grounds this was done, but the Duke of Elchingen caused the Gallimard edition to be impounded almost at once, though luckily or unluckily (unluckily in the Duke's view, luckily in mine, since I had already received two copies) not before a great many had been sold. The most powerful of French publishing houses had been outbid by the firm, till then mainly known for its *curiosa*, of Jean-Jacques Pauvert, which began putting out its own comprehensive Roussel the following year, in eye-catching scarlet covers.

There is, I fear, to this day some rivalry between two groups of Roussel exponents in France, in essence those of the *surréaliste* old guard and the faction of the *nouveau roman*. I shall hope to offend neither group in any fundamental way, though I would venture criticisms on both sides and could only wish that the comical differences might be reconciled. I did not think so very highly of M. Foucault's book, though it had its redeeming features. I found M. Robbe-Grillet's eventual article on Roussel, in the December 1963 *Critique*, disappointing and have since wondered, all-uncharitably, whether he could have been annoyed by the victory of the *surréaliste* old guard. For these, in the person of M. Ferry, are in command of the Pauvert edition and have enlisted Mr. Ashbery. I must, on the other hand, say both that I am an admirer of M. Robbe-Grillet and that I have sometimes thought M. Ferry's comments (on both MM. Robbe-Grillet and Foucault) charged with a quite unsuitable acerbity. As to M. Pauvert, he has in recent years showed himself to be a really exciting publisher, which does not mean that I have anything against the house of Gallimard.

Of course, none of all this ought to concern us Anglo-Saxons at all. Here we all are, even the totally monoglot among us, almost in a position to decide whether the name of Raymond Roussel is or is not one which is going to mean something to us. In making our decision, the last thing we want to be distracted by is literary politics in Paris. If we take note of French critical opinion at all, these are bound to be obtruded upon us, but let us try to be at least as straightforward and independent as we have in general contrived to be about Proust.

II

THE EARLY POEMS AND STORIES

As we are most likely to meet it now, *Mon Âme* occurs as a kind of appendix to the volume *Nouvelles Impressions d'Afrique*, the first and last works in verse first appearing together in volume form, in 1932, thirty-five years after the first appearance of *Mon Âme* in a periodical, the Sunday *Gaulois*, and about thirty-eight after its composition. It is a not-unimpressive work, and Raymond Roussel continued to think highly of it all his life.

When it appeared in a book with the *Nouvelles Impressions*, its title had been altered. It had become *L'Âme de Victor Hugo*. The original poem had been newly prefaced with the brief explanation that, one night, the poet had dreamt that he saw Victor Hugo writing at his work table and that the poem which follows was what he read when he looked over Victor Hugo's shoulder. The penultimate stanza reads:

> *À cette explosion voisine*
> *De mon génie universel,*
> *Je vois le monde qui s'incline*
> *Devant ce nom:* Victor Hugo.

From the rhyme-pattern, it is clear that the name of Raymond Roussel stood in the first place where that of Victor Hugo now stands and that it was to *his* universal genius the world bowed. Perhaps one day it will transpire when the alteration was made, whether when, in 1897, it first became clear that Roussel's *'génie universel'* was not to be acknowledged straightaway or when, thirty-five years later, still disappointed of his expectations, he arranged the volume, *Nouvelles Impressions d'Afrique*, for publication. In any case, the self-identification with Victor Hugo was not casually improvised at that moment, whatever the moment was.

The poet's soul is a factory, a mine, a rhyme-producing furnace. He rides on horseback about his domain, which is on the coast and contains a harbour capable of taking ocean-going vessels. He encourages his workmen and greets shiploads of admiring visitors. At night, the flames generally die down, but sometimes in a nightmare they flare up again, and the rhyme-factory produces wild fantasies and nonsense. At other times, the work may go on calmly through the night.

That is pretty well all the poem says. A single image is sustained and elaborated throughout, though in the nightmare section we may note the halbardiers and the pair of lovers who arouse the restless poet's jealousy, the woman a dark-eyed Spanish beauty holding out her arms to him. This is the first of many counter-indications in Roussel's work to M. Leiris's firm statement that his taste was exclusively homosexual. It is, of course, possible that we should always suppose there to have been a Proustlike substitution of girl for boy or blending of girl and boy.

It is perhaps in *La Doublure* that we are most quickly led to think of Proust in connection with Roussel. As in *À l'Ombre des Jeunes Filles en Fleur*, the action takes place largely at the sea-side. Like Marcel's Albertine, Gaspard's Roberte leaves him. We do not, alas, know whether Roberte had any 'original', boy or girl. We do know that Proust read *La Doublure* in 1897.

La Doublure is described on the title-page and cover not as a *roman en vers* but quite simply as a *roman*. In view of the more important slip of paper pasted into a later printing of the *Impressions d'Afrique*, recommending us to read the second half first, it may at least momentarily amuse us that a note at the beginning of *La*

Doublure states that, as the poem is a novel, it should be started at the first page and finished on the last.

The poem-novel is in six parts. The first and last parts show Gaspard alone, in theatrical costume, first at the end of a performance, finally before one. An unsuccessful actor, in the first part he has once more bungled his performance, as understudy, in a respectable theatre. In the last part, going downhill, he is about to perform in a sub-theatrical performance at a fair. His costume in the last part is that of Mephistopheles, as was to be the actor's costume with which we are much concerned in *Chiquenaude*, the first-published (three years after the publication of *La Doublure*) of the prose stories, which makes play with the word '*doublure*' as meaning, on the one hand, an understudy and, on the other, the lining of a garment. Much later, in *Comment J'Ai Écrit Certains de mes Livres*, Roussel was to state explicitly, however, that in *La Doublure* there is no trace of the kinds of underlying word-play he was presently to adopt. Still, there was always a preoccupation with theatrical false-face, one appearance concealing and thus, as we might say, being lined with another, which in its turn may be expected to conceal further appearances.

The idea is certainly vivid in parts three and four of *La Doublure*, which make up the greater part of the volume. For some two thousand alexandrine couplets, Gaspard and his Roberte, themselves masked, thread their way, armed with satchels of confetti and little shovels, among the crowd on an afternoon of carnival in Nice. Nothing important to their story happens, but a ceaseless variety of little encounters and passing shows is described. Eyes glitter behind masks or through holes in the necks of pasteboard heads. It is excessive, and one tires of it. Perhaps one tires more rapidly because it is all in verse and all in the same kind of verse. In a very substantial novel, one could perhaps accept so much description of the behaviour of individuals and groups in a crowd on holiday, especially if some of it bore on the development of a story. Victor Hugo, for instance, in *Notre Dame de Paris*, spends a good many pages on the milling around of medieval crowds (pages which, with Roussel's known feeling for Hugo, we may reasonably suspect of having inspired him to a comparable effort). But *Notre Dame* is a much longer work than *La Doublure*, and what happens at the festival there carries the story forward, whereas the carnival sequence in *La Doublure* takes up considerably more than half the book and merely postpones the story. Certainly, we need to know that the lovers were at Nice in carnival time, but their idyll was not confined to that one afternoon, and, apart from an evening of mild but happy sensuality before their departure from Paris and the evening of that same day of carnival, spent delightfully down by the sea, the other scenes of that idyll go unrecorded, while Roberte's eventual defection is merely recalled by Gaspard in the last part, while he sits miserably, made up as Mephistopheles, in a booth at the fair in Neuilly.

The carnival images were to persist. More than five years after the publication of *La Doublure*, Roussel wrote (and published in *Le Gaulois du Dimanche*) two poems, *L'Inconsolable* and *Têtes de Carton du Carnaval de Nice*, both again in alexandrine couplets, the one of some eight hundred lines, the other of more than a hundred, which could both have been inserted *in toto* in the carnival sequence of *La Doublure*. A certain amount of harking back to earlier work is common enough among writers, but this is truly remarkable. The description in verse of a carnival must have seemed to Roussel to be a major undertaking indeed and his first effort, despite its great length, to have somehow lacked a desirable completeness.

With all the reservations one has to make, I find *La Doublure* a deeply moving work. Roussel was never again to be straight-forwardly moving in that way, essentially the way of 'realistically' putting us in possession of the facts of a simple human story, that of a happy but temporary love in the life of a bad but uncomplaining actor, which may be presumed to have moved the author himself, precisely, it may be, at the fair in Neuilly, where he lived. It is strange that a work composed in the mood of exaltation Janet depicts should be sensitively concerned with failure. It is perhaps also strange that the first full-scale work of a rich young man should be centred upon a man, apparently no longer young, whose life is so markedly affected by economic pressures. In no general way was Raymond Roussel ever to show himself interested in social problems or pre-occupied with the alleviation of modern distress.

A minor point we may note is that the narration in *La Doublure* is conducted wholly in the present tense, as it is also in *L'Inconsolable* and *Têtes de Carton*. It is perhaps a point of more importance that, in so far as a foreigner can judge, Roussel was, from the outset, extraordinarily well-equipped, technically, as a poet. He did not, it is true, attempt any great variety of forms, but what seem to be exemplary alexandrines are added to each other without apparent effort, always lucid, uncontorted, not much padded with the usual *chevilles*, the prose sense carried forward with what, I dare say, might be considered too much *enjambement*, all, in its own odd way, very modern and simple on the surface. But, on the surface, Roussel is rarely obscure.

The title-piece in the volume *La Vue* is a poem of some two thousand lines. The volume contains two further poems, *Le Concert* and *La Source*, of about half that length. Each describes, in far more detail than it is possible to imagine being physically visible, a miniature view. In *La Vue*, it is a sea-side prospect engraved on a lens set into a penholder. In *Le Concert*, it is the heading of a sheet of hotel writing paper, showing the hotel itself, an omnibus standing before it, the lake beyond and public gardens with a band-stand. In *La Source*, the label on a bottle of mineral water shows the spring itself and a girl in peasant costume serving customers with the wholesome draught.

In *La Vue*, we gather of the poet's own situation only that he is standing by a window and that the view in the lens evokes for him a holiday season spent at the resort there depicted. He has never been to the hotel in *Le Concert*, but the letter is in a feminine hand dear to him, and he is reading it, for the hundredth time, at midnight. In *La Source*, he is lunching at a restaurant in which are also a young and an older couple, a white-bearded man reading a newspaper and a pale, lanky American who leans back on his chair. The bottle of mineral water is finally whisked off the table by a waiter, who has brought the poet his long-awaited dish. The whole of the rest of each poem describes in impossible detail the miniature scene and the numerous people in it. Their facial expressions are distinctly perceived. We know what each is doing and even, to some extent, what each is thinking or saying. We do not know what the band is playing, but we do know what kind of tone they are producing, and we know that the two ladies on the balcony are English.

The game is not unamusing, and these are shapely poems. At one time, it may be remembered, M. Robbe-Grillet and his contemporaries were known as the *école du regard*. Insofar as mere looking and closely describing is a principal characteristic of their works, *La Vue* may well have been the volume of Roussel's which most affected them. In M. Robbe-Grillet's own fourth novel, *Dans le Labyrinthe*, moreover, there is a repeated suggestion that the action merely derives from a picture on the wall. I understand, from M. Robbe-Grillet himself, that his second novel, *Le Voyeur*, was in the first place to have been called *La Vue*.

In the posthumous volume, *Comment J'Ai Écrit Certains de mes Livres*, the seventeen earliest stories are grouped together as *Textes de Grande Jeunesse ou Textes-Genèse*. The collocation of the two near-homophones '*jeunesse*' and '*genèse*' is no mere example of the punning word-play which was to underpin most of Roussel's work in prose. In the order in which these seventeen stories are printed, the first three are truly *textes-genèse* in a sense which I hope will presently appear, and the suggestion perhaps is that, primitive as they must be considered, they were written a little later than the others, *i.e.*, not in what Roussel regarded as his extreme youth.

All seventeen of them and a number of somewhat later pieces display a strict and invariable formula. The opening phrase of each story is repeated at the end of it, with the change (or omission or addition) of only one letter or (in a single case) one consonantal sound which requires the addition of two letters. The rest of the phrase remains identical to eye and ear. There are, that is to say, no differently spelt homophones or differently pronounced homographs, though other nouns in the phrase may be taken in different senses. Thus *Parmi les Noirs*, the story printed first, begins:

Les lettres du blanc sur les bandes du vieux billard formaient un incompréhensible assemblage.

It ends with the incomprehensible array of characters in chalk round the edges of a worn billiard table being rearranged to read:

LES . . . LETTRES . . . DU . . . BLANC . . . SUR . . . LES . . .
BANDES . . . DU . . . VIEUX . . . PILLARD.

This is intended as a compliment to one of the guests, an explorer, whose recent book, *Parmi les Noirs*, consisted, precisely, of the letters of a white man on the armed bands of an aged but predatory black chieftain.

In the second story, '*les anneaux du gros serpent à sonnettes*' (the coils of the big rattlesnake) become, at the end, '*les anneaux du gros serpent à sonnets*' (a pair of ear-rings given to the narrator, who had saved him from what must have been rather a boa constrictor than a rattlesnake, by a sonnet-writing big man, a player upon the brass musical instrument known as a serpent). The opening and closing phrases of ensuing stories are '*les taches de la laine sur le gros mouton à cinq pattes*' and '. . . *gros bouton à cinq pattes*', '*les tours de la mèche autour du bâton du cerceau*' and '. . . *du berceau*', '*le haut de la figure avec le bout de craie du tableau*' and '. . . *raie du tableau*'. And so on. There is no great naturalness about any of these phrases in either their concluding or their initial forms and meanings, so that we hardly know at which end to suppose that Roussel's imagination began. In some cases, we hardly know, at the outset, just what meaning is to be given to the initial statement itself, though it quickly transpires. What we know with certainty is that he devised his two variants and then made up a story to bridge the distance between them.

All the stories are told in the first person, and in most of them it is the narrator who, at the end, triumphantly produces the altered phrase, though in no case can his auditors know in what the triumph consists, since they are unaware of what the phrase originally was. A number of characters recur, the rich Goulots, the elderly mathematics teacher Volcan, the painter Dabussol, but this recurrence tells us little about the order in which the stories were written or about any significance in the order in which they are printed. The three printed first are three that were to be rehandled, are in that sense *textes-genèse*, the start of something. The quality of the other tales varies considerably. An element of monotony in the group as a whole is provided by the fact that in no fewer than ten of the stories we are concerned with some painting or drawing, a wrong detail in which generally provides the pay-off lines themselves. Certain words recur ('*sonnettes*', '*raie*', '*bouton*', '*boucle*'). In two stories, there is what appears to be unintended confusion, as though Roussel had simply forgotten what he had told us earlier. Games and practical jokes abound. They are rarely amusing in themselves.

We must remember, however, that Roussel himself did not think well of any of these seventeen early stories and made no attempt to print any of them when they were first written. His reason for including them in the posthumous *Comment J'Ai* was purely to document the earliest, simplest and most open of his verbal procedures. Yet several of the stories are fine or contain fine things. The seventh, for instance, gives us a balloon ascent in which the receding landscape is beautifully rendered. No doubt there is some debt here to Jules Verne, but it is likely enough that the rich and leisured Raymond Roussel occasionally chartered a balloon. A further marked virtue of this story is that the opening and closing lines ('*les boucles du petit rentier tout blanc*' and '. . . *petit sentier tout blanc*') are more integrally part of the total impression than is common elsewhere, the question being one of distinguishing, from a great height, the balloonists' white-haired host on a winding path far below.

There is also something curiously pleasing about the thirteenth and sixteenth stories. The earlier of these starts with a poem, too

good to have been written by the boy of eleven to whom it is
attributed:

> *Qui n'a pas vu la frange d'or*
> *De la petite Paulette*
> *Ne peut pas se douter encor*
> *De ce qu'est une fillette. . . .*

As so often, a portrait is involved, and it is in this case a detail only
apparently wrong with it which gives us in conclusion the altered
form of the poem's first two lines ('. . . *la frange d'or de la petite
épaulette*') with, unusually, no other word receiving a secondary
meaning, since a little girl's hair and the depicted shoulder-piece of
a military uniform may equally be said to have a golden fringe. As so
often elsewhere in Roussel's work, the sixteenth is a story within a
story. It renders in words effects of light and perspective not easily
so rendered. Legend and contemporary episode are naturally and
charmingly mingled, and the word-play itself (as between '*rayon
vert*' and '*crayon vert*' and with the two senses of '*la peau de la raie*' as
a fish's scales and as the scalp visible along a parting in the hair) is
both natural-seeming and ingenious.

The most impressive of all the seventeen earliest stories, however,
is to my mind the fourteenth, which takes us from '*la peau verdâtre
de la prune un peu mûre*' to '*la peau verdâtre de la brune un peu mûre*'.
Again, the other words do not change meaning. The aging Spanish
beauty's complexion has turned greenish as a result of poison
administered by way of a ripening plum.[1] This story is unique, in
Roussel's writing, for a type of ambiguity which, I suggest, has
proved fruitful in the work of M. Robbe-Grillet. Superficially, it
is recalled only by the last-printed and last-written of the prose
sketches, *La Chambre Secrète*, in M. Robbe-Grillet's *Instantanés*, itself
quite unique in M. Robbe-Grillet's work. In both cases, all that is
described is the death of a woman, apparently at the hands of a
former lover, and the latter's withdrawal from the scene. The
extreme, romantic theatricality of both scenes itself constitutes the

[1] See Appendix.

28

ambiguity. M. Robbe-Grillet's withdrawal is slow-motion cinematographic, but then so are his minute portrayals of scenes from what is clearly intended to be real life. Roussel's story is told, like the other sixteen, in the first person, and, until we think about it afterwards, we remain uncertain whether the narrator is to be regarded as a real-life poisoner or as an actor playing a poisoner's part on the stage. The effect is powerful and certainly deliberated. Among the products of the years of mere 'prospecting' this one shows a vein we might well have wished Roussel himself should exploit. The fact that he did not exploit it is surprising in view of his continuing tendency to dwell upon matters involved in theatrical performance.

Of the three stories printed first in order among those seventeen '*textes de grande jeunesse ou textes-genèse*,' *Parmi les Noirs* was, as Roussel tells us, to provide a framework for his largest prose work, *Impressions d'Afrique*. Rehandled, the next two become *Nanon* and *Une Page de Folk-Lore Breton*. In his posthumous volume, these are printed in the '*citations documentaires*' section, where they are preceded by the story *Chiquenaude* and followed by the two poems, *L'Inconsolable* and *Têtes de Carton du Carnaval de Nice*, and more remotely by the 'Martial' pages from Janet and by Tartakower's articles on Roussel's contribution to chess theory. Of *Chiquenaude* Roussel tells us, in the introductory essay, that it was the only one of his early stories to please him. It was the only one he published (in the *Gaulois du Dimanche* in 1900). More verse and further 'prospecting' followed, and Roussel began to feel, by the age of thirty, that he had found his way in prose. The elaborated *Nanon* and *Une Page de Folk-Lore Breton* then appeared in the Sunday *Gaulois* in 1907 and the following year.

Like the seventeen earliest stories, *Chiquenaude* opens with a sentence ('*Les vers de la doublure dans la pièce du* Forban talon rouge *avaient été composés par moi*') of which the substantive part appears transmogrified at the end (as '*les vers de la doublure dans la pièce du fort pantalon rouge*', with '*vers*' as verses becoming '*vers*' as clothes mites). The story of the play is of an invulnerable Mephisto rendered vulnerable by a bad fairy on behalf of her swashbuckling godson, presumably the red-heeled buccaneer of a title nevertheless mainly chosen to yield its atrocious pun. Mephisto is played that evening by an understudy ('*doublure*'). It is his garments which make him invulnerable, and, while he is without them, the fairy godmother and a ballet of her colleagues pick out the lining ('*doublure*') and get moth into it. This is sad stuff, and it is difficult to see why Roussel preferred *Chiquenaude* to all his previous ventures in prose, though it is longer and more elaborate than the seventeen earliest stories. Gaspard, it may be remembered, at the end of the long poem *La Doublure* wears the red garb of a stage Mephistopheles and was at first seen as an understudy, but Roussel himself has told us that we must not look for any significant link between poem and story.

In *Nanon*, we are again concerned with the coils of the big rattle-snake and the ear-rings of the sonnet-writing player upon the serpent. The latter's tragic love-story is much dwelt on, the whole piece being now more than twice as long. The third of the seventeen stories had originally contained a good deal of verse, supposedly parts of a poem by the narrator which an artist friend is illustrating. In *Une Page de Folk-Lore Breton*, the poem appears in full at a length of some thousand lines. Its legendary background is attributed to the sonnet-writing player upon the serpent, himself a Breton. The outrageous verbal transformation of a miracle-working five-legged sheep into a 'bouton *à cinq pattes*' (a button holding together five strands of cloth, all that remain of the wonder-boy's original costume) still provides us with our opening and conclusion. It is the poem itself which provides *Une Page de Folk-Lore Breton* with all its interest. The original story, with its verse inserts, has become essentially a poem of some length, with brief prologue and epilogue in prose. These display for the last time the first of Raymond Roussel's verbal procedures, an opening phrase reappearing modified at the end, the two linked by a story. The formula's chief disadvantage was that it stood open to inspection. Roussel was now to adopt two varieties of a concealed verbal procedure, about which very little could have been guessed but for the posthumous revelation of *Comment J'Ai*.

It may be worth insisting at this point that in none of the many early stories can the anguish of a neurotic personality be readily perceived. But, indeed, nowhere in his work does Raymond Roussel strike one as a writer driven to seek expression for deeply buried impulses. All persistent writers and creative artists are perhaps acting under some form of compulsion, and, in one sense of the word, Raymond Roussel was a 'compulsive' writer. I take it, however, that in the main he was simply compelled to pursue an activity he enjoyed and one in which he felt at home, as he rarely did in the world outside. He was driven to create a world, recognisedly unreal but full of order, a world governed by arbitrary and controllable rules, a world of play, a world in large measure innocent. It seems to me particularly true of the early stories. In them, we are recurrently aware of a tenderness felt especially towards little girls. If we except the melodramatic and theatrical poisoning of the '*brune un peu mûre*', the worst that happens is that one or two practical jokes begin to look as if they might get out of hand.

But nowhere in Raymond Roussel is the human climate oppressive. In *Impressions d'Afrique*, we shall find that crimes are committed and that discovered criminals are subjected to torture. But the point of the tortures is their ingenuity and appropriateness. Pain, bloodshed and convulsive reactions are nowhere paraded for our delectation. We may wonder at the severity with which the black lovers, Naïr and Jizme, are punished, since they had principally offended Mossem, himself condemned, but in all other cases the sentence is just and may be avoided if the victim repents. The crimes themselves were, for the most part, acts of oppression and treachery committed for greed against the inoffensive and helpless, who also frequently are young.

III

IMPRESSIONS OF AFRICA

A SHIP ON its way from Marseilles to Buenos Aires is wrecked upon the African coast. Its varied and distinguished passenger list includes musicians, scientists, artists and *artistes*, circus freaks and bankers. They are conducted to Ejur, capital of the black emperor, Talu VII. He requires large ransom, and an envoy, who in his youth had travelled to Europe, is despatched. Pending his return, the passengers set up organisations of their own and devote themselves largely to the devising and rehearsal of a remarkable gala performance, for which they also obtain massive local participation, including that of the Emperor himself. For him, the occasion further becomes that of his ritual self-investment as king of a territory conquered by him during the stay of the Europeans.

Impressions d'Afrique in fact opens with the investiture, the punishment of certain traitors and the gala performance, and it is not until page 212 (of the Lemerre edition, page 147 in Pauvert, page 152 of the English translation) that the anonymous narrator begins reminiscently to describe the preceding events, an account which takes him to page 452, three further pages then sufficing to return the travellers to Europe and to round off the book. M. Foucault rightly stresses a tendency in Roussel first to mystify, then to explain, a tendency not only in particular works but throughout the general course of his life and work, ending posthumously with the key provided by *Comment J'Ai Écrit Certains de mes Livres*. There are signs, nevertheless, of Roussel possibly wondering later whether, in *Impressions d'Afrique*, he might not have overdone it, as he was certainly not to do in the succeeding *Locus Solus* or the two plays.

In the dramatic version of 1911–12, all is presented in chronological order, as we may see from the one actor's part salvaged by John Ashbery and printed, in 1964, in the special Roussel number of *Bizarre*. In the *Pages Choisies* of 1918, what we are offered from *Impressions d'Afrique* is simply its second half, with the chapters, originally X to XXVI, renumbered I to XVII and the sentence, on the original page 212, with which the protracted flashback opens, altered to begin, '*Le 15 mars 19 . . .*', not, as it had formerly begun, '*Le 15 mars précédent*'. In a fourth impression of the full text, dated 1932, a slip has been pasted, on which those unfamiliar with the art of Raymond Roussel are recommended to read pages 212–455 first and pages 1–211 subsequently, a recommendation of which no mention is made by M. Ferry in the current edition.

True, Roussel made no attempt to reshape the whole book in print, either in his lifetime or, so far as we know, by leaving instructions with Lemerre's master-printer for any posthumous reissue. Still, it may seem worth pointing out that, although *Impressions d'Afrique* was three times reprinted in Roussel's lifetime, the type had not been reset (except, half of it, for the *Pages Choisies*), nor was the book reprinted in its original form after his death. We cannot be perfectly certain that instructions for a posthumous reissue were not in fact left at Lemerre's, where certain of Roussel's last instructions appear to have been demonstrably ignored. We do know that resetting would have put Roussel to some expense, and, according to his nephew Michel Ney, by 1932 the money was running out, as were the sands. It would have been too naïve on Roussel's part to imagine that his printed slip really would persuade readers to begin reading at page 212, go on to the end and then turn back to the beginning. The printed slip may have been something of a despairing gesture. It would, in any case, have been more reasonable to recommend first reading pages 212–452, then 1–211, then the final chapter.

For the benefit of a few strong-minded readers, it may here be said that, in the English translation, this would mean first reading pages 152–315, then 5–151, then 316–7. Hereinafter, all page-references will be to the English translation.

When I first undertook that translation in collaboration with Lindy Foord, I wondered if we ought not to follow those later indications of Roussel's and present all in chronological order, as I felt he might finally have wished. In the end, of course, this was not done. The decision not to do it was perhaps uncourageous. Certainly, I had reason to expect critical disapprobation in France and from the knowledgeable few here. But then perhaps also a writer's later disquietudes about his book must be regarded as of less account than his original conception. And so the book stands as it was, for better or worse.

It has already been said that the early story, *Parmi les Noirs*, provided a framework for *Impressions d'Afrique* and was truly a *texte-genèse* in that sense. This, it may be remembered, is the story which begins with '*les lettres du blanc sur les bandes du vieux billard*' and ends with '*les lettres du blanc sur les bandes du vieux pillard*', almost identical phrases in which every noun has changed its meaning.

Among the talented passengers on the *Lynceus* is a sopranist, Carmichael. His act, which he had hoped to popularise in America, was typically performed in a golden wig and a blue gown with a long train. Embroidered on this train is the number 472, sewn there by a drunken companion, it being the lucky number drawn by Carmichael when registering for military service. Such numbers have, in French popular life since Napoleonic times, enjoyed a fetichistic importance to which I know of no equivalent here and may be seen in heavily embroidered form in museums and doubtless among family heirlooms. In due course, the Emperor (the '*vieux pillard*') is much taken with Carmichael's costume and reveals an unexpected talent for singing falsetto, in which the European visitor (a '*blanc*' in the second sense) is made to coach him. We shall find

Talu VII wearing the wig and the dress with the long train in the battle against Yaour IX, by which his kingdom is enlarged.

A billiard cue is a *queue*, and so is the train of a gown. A billiard cue is frequently marked with a number or with its owner's initials. From the *reprises* or darning in old and mended *bandes* (not those of a billiard table) Raymond Roussel's associative mental processes moved to the *reprises* (in a musical sense) of the interminably repetitive epic chant of the *bandes* of Ponukelian warriors. Carmichael, ordered to learn this by heart for the gala performance, will break down. He will then be locked up for three hours until he is word-perfect. The association here, Roussel tells us, was between the *colle* which is paste or glue sticking paper to billiard chalk ('*blanc*' in the first sense) and the '*colle*' which in schoolboy slang formerly meant an imposition or detention. But, as any French reader may be expected to know at least subliminally, there is a wider pocket of word-associations here than Roussel himself seems to have held in full consciousness while writing his explanatory essay. For instance, there is an expression (for stump, flummox) '*coller sur bande*', while the word '*bande*' has its nautical uses, which '*reprise*' also has.

Thereafter, Roussel adopted two systematic forms of associative verbal procedure, one primarily semantic, the other phonic. It is with these, insofar as they bear on the composition of *Impressions d'Afrique* and insofar as Roussel has minutely indicated them in *Comment J'Ai Écrit Certains de mes Livres*, that some pages must now be concerned. Ideally, they are addressed to the reader who has already gone through *Impressions of Africa* innocently, as Gide, Vitrac and Cocteau went through *Impressions d'Afrique* innocently in their time. Indeed, the strong-minded reader who has picked up the present little book first by accident might at this point consider putting it down and taking up *Impressions of Africa*, giving me his esteemed further attention again later.

In the book, Seil Kor is first seen as a pitiable madman upon whom a strange therapy is practised at the investiture and gala. We presently learn that he is Talu's interpreter, with whose youthful stay in Europe had been connected a tragic story of the death of his white patron's adored daughter. Much later, we discover that it was Seil Kor who had first met the shipwrecked party and that shortly thereafter he had been despatched to Europe to collect their ransom. His disturbed state is due to head injuries he has received since his return to Ejur and not long before the gala performance, during which one of the former passengers on the *Lynceus* cures him by hallucinatingly re-enacting the painful but also blissful story in all its apparent reality. In the chronological order of things, Seil Kor's story had been the first thing recounted to the European travellers, before they moved inland to Ejur and while the damaged ship was being unloaded.

Seil Kor's story is to be found on pages 137–68 of *Impressions of Africa*. We must, I think, assume that it had been written before those pages, 104–9, in which the young negro is cured of his mental disorder at the gala. In its main outlines, we may suppose the story to have been spontaneously engendered by the imagination of Raymond Roussel. There had to be an interpreter. No doubt he had at one time travelled in Europe. How had this come about? Nothing could be more natural than that in youth he should have been taken up by a benevolent French explorer. What was his story? Nothing would more readily present itself to Roussel's imagination than blissful companionship with a fair-haired little girl, ending tragically. This little girl would presumably be the explorer's daughter, and it might well be that her death (a Freudian might say, Germaine Roussel's marriage) would be a thing for which Seil Kor felt himself to be responsible and that it should later, under stress, lie at the heart of a temporary madness in him. Stripped of its theatrical trappings, even the mode of cure is decidedly on psycho-analytical lines, since it is effected by once more bringing a painfully buried memory into full consciousness.

Many details of the story, however, were supplied by a verbal procedure which consisted in taking two nouns, each susceptible of more than one meaning, and linking them together by means of the general-purpose preposition *à*. Picked in the first place to make sense together, each of the two nouns is subsequently taken in a remoter meaning, Roussel's imagination then making what it could of the result. As psycho-analysis has been mentioned, it may be worth pointing out here that the procedure allowed an absolute minimum of free association, was positively counter-Freudian. We do not know precisely how Roussel selected his words. We do know that he was addicted to poring over dictionaries. We do not know just how rigorously, once two words had been paired, he felt bound to abide by the result, however unpromising it might seem. On the other hand, certain of the results appear so forced that we may well be inclined to suppose that the rules of the game did not allow any pair of words, once joined, to be rejected or reshuffled. The oddest cases, however, are not found in Seil Kor's story. Of word-pairing in connection with the genesis of this story, Roussel gives us ten examples, recalled more than twenty years later.

'*Tulle à pois*' is a not unnatural collocation of words and is indeed found in use as meaning the kind of spotted net of which a veil is made. There is also a French town, Tulle, the departmental capital of Corrèze, and on a map it may be indicated by a '*pois*' in the sense of a large dot. Not unnaturally, during the two years of their travels together, the explorer, Laubé, has passed some of the time in teaching Seil Kor the elements of French history and geography, and they are running through departments and prefectures by way of revision before Laubé presents to his wife and daughter the black boy whose learnedness he has described to them. The explorer has just asked Seil Kor for the principal town of Corrèze when Laubé's daughter appears in the hotel gardens and is seen by Seil Kor who, dazzled, cannot answer, so that the name of Tulle will for ever thereafter remain engraved on his memory.

This childish love at first sight takes place in Tripoli, a not unnatural choice of meeting-place for the Laubés after their long separation, but perhaps finally decided upon by Roussel after dictionary browsings had given him '*martingale à tripoli*' as meaning a piece of harness and the rottenstone with which it is polished. The reader unfamiliar with stables, who may already feel that there is more French here than he cares to learn, may console himself with the fact that he is also learning his own language, for both terms are in English use in those senses, as is 'martingale' in the sense of a gambling system. At the casino in Tripoli, Seil Kor, by doubling his stakes in that way, wins enough to buy a spectacular cake for Nina's party.

These two examples affect pages 158–60 of *Impressions of Africa*. On pages 164–5, we find the two children, now in France, on a rainy day, playing in a coach-house or cart-bay, mimicking what they had seen the previous evening at a circus performance in the village. Nina makes out of two hand-bills a mask and a cap, and out of the covers of some copies of the magazine *Nature* a ruff, for Seil Kor. They dance a bolero. The word-pairs involved were '*loup à griffes*' (a wolf and its claws becoming a domino mask made from a sheet of paper printed with signatures), '*fraise à nature*' (the ruff,) '*feuille à tremble*' (an aspen leaf becoming the other hand-bill, headed, 'Tremble, people of France') and '*boléro à remise*' (no longer a cut-price short jacket but danced in the coach-house). Sweating from the dance, Nina catches a chill and from '*quinte à résolution*' as a musical notion has a fit of coughing while doing her catechism. Her blue frock and the bed of moss on which she falls asleep on the first night of Advent have verbal origins of the same kind, and so, at the gala performance, does the projecting roof beneath which the hypnotist Darriand recreates his therapeutic illusions.

Of the material given him by this word-pairing, the story of Seil Kor and Nina is documented in most detail by Roussel. He gives us, however, thirty-seven other examples applicable to *Impressions d'Afrique*. To set all these out in such a way as to make them intelligible to a possibly monoglot English reader would take up a great deal of space and might be tedious. A case which aroused particular derision at performances of the stage version was that of the helot's statue in corset whalebone trundled along lines made of animal tissue. This started with three pairs of words, '*baleine à îlot*', '*duel à accolade*' and '*mou à raille*', which I forbear to analyse. A pair which yielded a piece of dialogue I find amusing was '*arlequin à salut*', which, on page 13 of the translation, gives us:

'Waiter, what is all that ringing of bells?'
'It's for Benediction.'
'Right, bring me a plate of scraps.'

I suppose that Roussel found it amusing, but it is not quite possible to be sure.

For the gala performance, six *tableaux vivants* have been devised, each illustrating a story. In respect of two of the stories, Roussel has left us detailed clues as to the verbal procedure he next evolved. One of the stories (enacted on pages 76–8, told on 229–33) is that of a bewitchment on the shores of Lake Ontario. The deviser of the *tableaux vivants*, Soreau, a comedian and, apparently, operetta producer, about whom we are otherwise told little, is supposed to have picked it up in Quebec during a tour of North America. A little girl, Ursula, whose father has just died, is about to be drowned in the lake by her stepmother, with the help of the stepmother's sister and two brothers, when an Indian magician turns the wicked four into, respectively, a she-ass, a goose, a pike and a man with a boar's head. It is the gentle-natured Ursula herself who, after repeated efforts, does what must with great difficulty be done in order to restore them to human shape.

It is a pleasantly effective little story which might have arisen quite spontaneously in an imagination peopled with certain images. It might have been dreamt. It might have been some modification of an existing folk-tale. It has been described (by M. Butor) as a myth of the cyclical recurrence of the seasons. A preponderance of its concrete elements was in fact drawn, by phonic or phonetic association, from certain lines by Victor Hugo on a subject quite unrelated to that of the story.

These lines occur in a poem of some length on Napoleon II, from the volume *Les Chants du Crépuscule*. The lines, as they occur in Hugo's text, are as follows:

O revers! ô leçon!—Quand l'enfant de cet homme
Eut reçu pour hochet la couronne de Rome;
Lorsqu'on l'eut revêtu d'un nom qui retentit; . . .

Lorsqu'on eut pour sa soif posé devant la France
Un vase tout rempli du vin de l'espérance. . . .

As Roussel sets out the lines in *Comment J'Ai,* they are without punctuation or any indication of a break in the quotation after the third line, and there are two mistakes, each repeated, one of them of some little practical bearing. This is the substitution of '*quand*' for '*lorsque*' at the beginning of lines three and four. That for '*O/ô*' in the first line Roussel substituted '*Oh/oh*' serves merely to confirm that he was quoting from memory and that his memory was auditory, not visual.

Line by line, he sets out what elements of the story he recalls drawing from the lines of Hugo's poem. From '*Oh revers oh leçon . . . cet homme*' he derived the near-homophonic '*Or effet herse oh le son . . . séton*' and thus the gold or gilded portcullis, grille or other grating whose effect was to impede the transformed Gervaise's movements (with '*or*' perhaps also suggesting Ursule's fortune, for which the crime was to be committed), bran (but '*son*' appears exclamatorily, '*oh, le son!*' and may also have suggested the shindy kicked up by Gervaise and her family) and a suture or horse-doctor's subcutaneous dressing (typically a leather disc with a hole in the middle to drain pus, known to British veterinary surgeons as a rowel) which made the trough of bran inaccessible to the she-ass's mouth. From '*Eut reçu pour hochet la couronne de Rome*' came '*Ursule brochet lac Huronne drome (hippodrome)*' and from the ill-remembered '*Quand on l'eut revêtu*' '*Carton hure oeuf fétu*', while from '*pour sa soif posé devant*' we get '*pourchasse oie rose aide vent*'. Altogether, this gives us (gave Roussel), Ursula's name, a pike, a lake, a woman of the Huron tribe, the circular motion characteristic of the behaviour of animals in a circus ring, a pasteboard pig's snout ('*hure*', but a pike, a '*brochet*', also has one), an egg and a wisp of straw (two of the objects of markedly different weight the trans-

40

formed Claude was made to juggle with) and the driving of a goose by the wind with the help of a flailing rose-branch, which is what the stepmother's sister has to put up with.

According to the rules of his game, Roussel then had to construct a story incorporating all these elements. Free imagination still had its part to play. The procedure itself had named only one character, for instance. It was not clearly indicated that there should be transformation by magical means, though transformation of all kinds at all times preoccupied Raymond Roussel, and none would so readily seize on 'carton' as indicating a pasteboard head. That a father should die and his daughter be persecuted by a stepmother and her sister and two brothers, that Ursula should be of a sweetly forgiving nature or that she should be eight years old, were not laws binding imagination at the outset. There is Cinderella stuff here. Gervaise is the wicked stepmother, but she is an ugly sister as well, so ugly that she remained a spinster at twenty-five. The expression used for remaining a spinster is 'coiffer sainte Catherine', and Catherine wheels may have reinforced the idea of circular motion, the pike swimming round the lake year after year at great speed, joined only once a year for a brief and crucial moment by the other driven creatures.

From the last line of the Hugo quotation came five elements of a further story, enacted on pages 78-9 and told on 233-6. In 1932, Roussel himself remembered only that 'Un vase tout rempli du vin de l'espérance' had formerly given him, by phonetic association, 'sept houx . . . rampe . . . lit . . . Vesper'. He had evidently forgotten (and no longer perceived) that in 'v(in de l') espérance' the name 'Haendel' pronounced in a French way may be heard between the initial and the remaining letters of 'Vesper'. In addition, he had seven sprigs of holly, a handrail or balustrade (but it could have been footlights, a sense of the word 'rampe' with which Roussel had been concerned before), the idea of reading (but perhaps also with the idea of bed, bedridden, therefore old and infirm, in the background) and the Latin word for evening, which might well have occurred in, if not as, the title of a musical work. Flats and sharps apart, seven notes are separately lettered within the octave.

Automatic methods of composition, at once deliberate and accidental, preoccupied the author, Raymond Roussel. Handel did indeed go blind in the evening of his life. He is nowhere on record as being one of Roussel's favourite composers, one, therefore, who might be particularly hoped to have composed according to principles like Roussel's, taking sprigs of holly to represent notes, each tied with a ribbon whose colours he could not see.

From a musical point of view, it may also be worth noting that any large-scale work conforming strictly to the conditions in the story must have been extremely monotonous. We may reasonably suppose the seven notes to have been those of a diatonic scale, from which no serious modulation would be possible, whatever, within the permissible harmonic framework of the time, might be done with the accompanying parts. The difficulties would have been no less with a chromatic theme covering only a part or parts of the octave, given that it had to recur like a present-day dodecaphonalist's more extended tone-row, yet according to rules essentially diatonic. The rules according to which Roussel evolved his story restricted him less. The story, moreover, is short.

There is one other story in *Impressions of Africa* to which Roussel has left us a detailed key. This is the Oriental tale which Fogar, the Emperor's eldest son, causes his photographic plants to film and project in colour. It is said to occur in an illustrated volume, *The Poet and the Morisco*, in the possession of one of the European captives. The phonically suggestive verse-background this time was not provided by Hugo but by two well-known nursery songs. To begin with:

> *J'ai du bon tabac dans ma tabatière,*
> *J'ai du bon tabac, tu n'en auras pas;*
> *J'en ai du frais et du tout râpé,*
> *Mais ce n'est pas pour ton fichu nez. . . .*

No doubt in different nurseries the words vary a little, but that was the version supplied by Roussel's unchecked memory. His auditory imagination drew upon it as follows. From the first line he took 'Jade tube onde aubade en mat (objet mat) à basse tierce'. The story, told on pages 259–65, does indeed begin with the jade spout of a fountain and with a morning serenade sung over an instrument which sounds a lower third to each note. The metal of which this instrument is made is described as '*terne*', which in sense is not far removed from '*mat*'. Roussel must certainly have decided beforehand that it should be an Oriental tale. Jade may suggest Baghdad, but in French '*J'ai d(u)*' does not at once suggest '*jade*'. As M. Foucault points out, Roussel's inward ear might well have given him other near-homophones. '*Geai, tue, péan, ta bacchante*', '*Jette, Ubu, honte à bas*' and '*J'aide une bonne abaque*' are alternatives M. Foucault offers us off the cuff to what was yielded by the first musical phrase of this pretty gavotte tune alone. No mere association of sounds gave us our three principal characters, Shahnijar, Ghiriz and Neddu, the rich but artistic merchant, the poet whom he employs to sing morning serenades and the Moorish wife to whom he sings them and with whom he at once falls in love and she with him.

In the evening, Shahnijar takes his wife out upon a sandy eminence to watch the sunset. Afterwards, the amorous Ghiriz kisses the imprints of her tiny feet. '*Tu n'en auras pas*' has been turned into '*dune en or à pas*'. '*J'en ai du frais et du tout râpé*' yields '*jaune aide orfraie édite oracle paie*', and so there follows an episode in which Ghiriz consults a Chinese (*i.e.*, yellow) soothsayer, who auspicates, rather in ancient Roman than in Chinese fashion, by observing the flight of a bird of prey, not specified as an osprey. '*Mais ce n'est pas pour ton fichu nez*' gives '*mets sonne et bafoue, don riche humé*', and so the culinary preparation whose mere sniffing would send Shahnijar to sleep, whereupon a magic formula would cause the dish itself to ring until he awoke, discomfited.

Then Roussel turned to another song, and from '*Au clair de la lune mon ami Pierrot*' he derived '*eau glaire (cascade d'une couleur de glaire) de là l'anémone à midi négro*', which might be thought to be stretching a point, phonetically. In 1932, Roussel remembered of his further sources for this story only that '*Ma chandelle est . . .*' had given him '*marchande zélée*'. There is, indeed, a devoted black slave who wakens the lovers towards noon, and they have spent the night among rare flowers, represented at the gala performance by one resembling a giant anemone, beside a waterfall not perhaps glairy but '*à reflets verts*'. There is a wayside seller of foodstuffs who becomes '*empressée*' when urgently appealed to and is described as '*zélée*' in her portrayal at the gala. We can only guess at the origin of the zebra upon whose back the lovers fled.

The filming and projection, by sensitive plants, of *The Poet and the Morisco* is part of Fogar's contribution to the gala. Fogar particularly delighted André Gide, who read aloud to his friends the pages describing Fogar's underwater adventures. Aged fifteen, Fogar is the one black character in *Impressions of Africa* who displays inventive genius, not mere powers of mimicry. He has a remarkable capacity for putting himself into a cataleptic trance, with suspended heart-beat and respiration. In this condition, he can spend long periods under water. From the subaqueous depths he brings up a variety of unusual forms of life, out of whose artificially stimulated tropisms he devises, against the festive day, a pageant of great strangeness and complexity. It is a pity Roussel has left us so few clues to the evolution of Fogar and his many activities. The spotlight ('*phare*') he can turn on even when in his self-induced cataleptic trance (the ingenious Chènevillot having provided an armature fitted into his armpit) came from the writing on the wall at Belshazzar's feast, the words we know, from *Daniel* 5, XXV, as MENE, MENE, TEKEL UPHARSIN, the presumed root of this last word being, however, given three verses later as PERES. The inscription comes out differently in French Bibles, and what Roussel took was '*Mane, thecel, pharès*', briefly glossed by Larousse as counted, weighed and divided. To Roussel it yielded '*manette aisselle phare*'. Hellstern, 5 place Vendôme, was a shoemaker patronised by Roussel. Out of his name and address was formed '*hélice tourne zinc plat se rend (devient) dôme*' and so the apparatus with cylinders and propeller on pages 133–4. '*Lupus*' was a disease before it meant a wolf.

The procedure is, as Roussel says, related to rhyme.

Ce procédé, en somme, est parent de la rime. Dans les deux cas il y a création imprévue due à des combinaisons phoniques.

C'est essentiellement un procédé poétique.

44

On the whole, poets in English have always been shy of letting it become known that rhyming itself often modified the imagery and content of their poems. It may even be that a puritanical objection to what must nevertheless happen has made our poets, not only in modern times, go in for 'blank' and otherwise unrhymed verse more than has commonly been the case in France. It is, we may care to remember, to an idol of Roussel's, Victor Hugo, that we attribute the outrageous couplet, rhyming exactly throughout its length:

> Gal, amant de la reine, alla, tour magnanime,
> Galamment de l'arène à la Tour Magne, à Nîmes.

That can hardly have been a matter of versifying a statement whose sense was already fully present to Hugo's mind. It must all have been worked backward from hearing somebody speak of going or being present 'à la Tour Magne, à Nîmes', a punning tendency built into the quick tongue at once supplying 'alla, tour magnanime', the mind then recalling Roman arenas in the neighbourhood and the desperate gallantry of gladiators. The name 'Gal' must have come last and certainly 'l'arène' before 'la reine'. There is a close connection between rhyming and punning. Not all rhymes are puns, but we may say that all puns are rhymes. The opening and closing phrases of Raymond Roussel's early stories had been at once puns and elaborate but imperfect rhymes of Hugolian richness. By and large, we may say that all rhymes work backwards and infect sense and imagery. But a clever choice of rhymes will not make good verse, and Roussel himself points out that you have to know how to make good use of what he calls his *procédé évolué*.

Thereafter, he was not to depart from it in his prose works, with a single, modified reversion (which he gives us) to the earlier word-pairing in *Locus Solus*. It is only, however, in connection with *Impressions d'Afrique* that he has left us much detail of how the procedure worked, stating, indeed, that he remembers little about its workings even in connection with *Locus Solus*. I stopped short on word-pairing. I think I had better set out and briefly analyse all the examples Raymond Roussel himself gives us of the operations of the more complex and interesting *procédé évolué* and, for the moment, those which affect *Impressions of Africa*. A straightforward translation of the relevant pages of the title-essay in *Comment J'Ai Écrit Certains de mes Livres* would, alas, for the English reader, soon bog itself down in footnotes more extensive than the text.

Not only poems and nursery songs were taken and submitted to aural transformation. Images and episodes were derived from (as we have seen) a tradesman's address, from the captions to drawings by Caran d'Ache, from the titles of books and from single phrases. I take single phrases first. On pages 97–9, three apparitions are derived from two phrases. '*Napoléon, premier empereur*', gave '*Nappe ollé ombre miettes hampe air heure*'. From the first four words of this result we get a tablecloth, persons crying, '*Olé!*' with shadow and crumbs and thus Spanish dancers on a table, the scene so vividly represented that even the bread-crumbs cast a visible shadow. A wind-clock in the land of Cockaigne is derived from the remaining '*hampe air heure*', '*hampe*' meaning various kinds of staff or handle and among them a flagpole. A half-naked man appears with a bird on his finger. 'The Prince de Conti', the sculptor and illusionist Fuxier announces, 'and his jay', and that is all, '*à geai Conti nu*' having come from the expression '*à jet continu*', though Roussel himself thought that something must have escaped his memory here.

On pages 25–8, '*valet de pied*', transformed into '*va laide pie*', has produced the performing magpie, nowhere described as ugly, which is attached to the fair Louise Montalescot. On pages 67–8, the name of some apparatus, 'Phonotypia', seen on an advertisement and turned into '*fausse note tibia*', was responsible for the one-legged Breton who plays (but not wrong notes) on a flute made from his own shin-bone. On page 109, the Roman chariot, whose wheels, in turning, sound a high C, the '*char*', in fact, '*qu'ut y est*', began its existence as a pork-butcher, which is childish riddling. The title of a story by Barbey d'Aurevilly, '*Rideau Cramoisi*', was transliterated, with no phonetic change, as '*rit d'ocre à moisi*' and accounts for the strange make-up and horrible rictus of the tragic actress Adinolfa on page 115. A book-title, *Les Inconséquences de Monsieur Drommel*, by Victor Cherbuliez, awkwardly and not at all points closely turned into '*Raisin qu'un Celte hante démon scie Eude Rome elle*', gives us three of Fuxier's representations on page 118, as well as their embodiment in grapes, and leaves us two unused syllables over.

There were, it appears, and no doubt they may still be found, a series of Caran d'Ache drawings on the theme: *Patientez un peu*. One, bearing the caption, '*Antichambre ministérielle*', showed a wretched man waiting interminably beside an usher. Roussel took '*Patience à anti-chambre ministérielle*' and made of it '*Patience* (in the sense of a button-stick) *à entiche ambre mine hystérique* (*mine qui se précipite vers . . . ambre, qui s'entiche de . . .*)'. Thence, on pages 45–54, a protracted description of the scientist Bex's two marvellous inventions, out of which he could have made millions had he not so disinterestedly pursued knowledge for its own sake.

That is the last item on this list. True, we are led to suppose that the stories behind three further *tableaux vivants* came from the same poem by Victor Hugo which yielded the bewitchment on Lake Ontario and Handel writing on the balustrade. These stories concern, respectively, the discovery of a criminal in seventeenth-century Russia, the Greek hero Canaris and a rose and the kleptomania of an Italian prince. The name of Canaris, we may be certain, was indeed put into Roussel's mind by Hugo, since the next poem but one in *Les Chants du Crépuscule* is an ode addressed to that hero. It may be that patient labour or lucky flashes of insight might tease out more from the remaining two hundred and eleven lines of the poem on Napoleon II, but it could hardly be in the order of certainty. There is a great deal to be done on Raymond Roussel by scholarship of the ordinary sort, but perhaps more which falls into the province of the skilled crossword-puzzle solver or the deviser of tricky charades and treasure-hunt clues.

IV

LOCUS SOLUS

Bᴇᴛᴡᴇᴇɴ *Impressions d'Afrique* and *Locus Solus* came the stage version
of the former. In this, as has been said, all was arranged in chronological order. *Locus Solus* appearing in 1914, the war intervened
between its publication and any possible stage adaptation, whether
by its author or by another hand. I imagine *Locus Solus* to have been
conceived and written with an eventual stage adaptation in mind.
Unlike *Impressions d'Afrique*, it has something of the order that would
be required for a stage presentation. This tends to make one feel that
it is more satisfactory, more beautiful, formally. In what I have said
about *Impressions d'Afrique* and Roussel's apparent later feeling that
the order of the chapters might have been changed, there is perhaps
also a suggestion that, formally, the book is unsatisfactory. But then,
if, with Mr. F. R. Leavis, we are in part to admire a book for the
complexity of its organisation, it must be said that the complexity
of a book's organisation is doubled if it may and should be read two
ways round.

I feel no doubt, in fact, that *Impressions d'Afrique* is Roussel's masterpiece or that it is, quite simply, a masterpiece. On the other hand,
if my fellow-Rousselians put in a claim for *Locus Solus*, I shall understand perfectly well what they mean. I am for richness, they for lucid
form. I may say that, had I been consulted about the adaptation of

Locus Solus for theatrical performance, I should have recommended its arrangement as a play in three acts, not five.

Its seven chapters conceal an effectual division into three parts. The middle chapter is by far the longest. It is a little longer than the first three chapters put together and substantially longer than the last three chapters put together.

Though described as a novel, *Locus Solus* has even less in the way of over-all narrative framework than *Impressions d'Afrique*. The narrative framework simply is that a group of visitors, including an unnamed first-person narrator, are taken round the ingenious marvels visible on the estate, at Montmorency, about twelve miles outside Paris, of Martial Canterel, rich scientist, magician and illusionist.

As in all the later prose works, including the plays, it is the individual stories told or re-enacted which are of interest. The best of these in *Locus Solus* are of a haunting charm and strangeness. The book is more static than *Impressions d'Afrique*. There is less interplay between the various groups of characters and ingenuities. This is, as it were, a gala performance without real occasion.

In the first chapter, we go, on a first Thursday in April, to that 'place apart' of the title which is the villa at Montmorency and its large grounds. The first marvel Canterel shows and explains to his guests is a piece of African mud-sculpture, which might, we may feel, have stood in the main square of Ejur (it came from Timbuctoo). Strangely connected with it is a Breton legend, concerned, like more than one of Roussel's stories but also like many genuine folk-tales, with gold, equally of Freudian and alchemic significance.

The second chapter is somewhat longer than the first. In it, we are shown a paviour's beetle or rammer suspended from a dirigible balloon and operating automatically to create a mosaic of variously discoloured teeth, which Canterel has his own method of painlessly extracting. The principal figure in the mosaic is a soldier of fortune. Canterel tells us the story of this ruffian's redemption by a Norwegian lady whom he had been paid to kidnap.

The story is admirable. The grotesque notion of a tooth mosaic executed by a suspended rammer comes from the collocation of words '*demoiselle à prétendant*', distorted to give us '*demoiselle*' (in the sense of a paving beetle) '*à reître en dents*', the only further modification recalled by Roussel being that, from '*prétendant refusé*', he took '*rêve usé*' and so the soldier of fortune's dream, which plays an important part in the story. The perhaps unfamiliar word '*reître*' comes from the German '*Reiter*', that kind of mounted soldier of fortune being characteristically a German product or thought so in medieval France.

This is, apparently, the only case in *Locus Solus* of an episode derived in part from a simple collocation of words, and even so one of the words is phonetically transmogrified. The rest is all evolved by way of the '*procédé évolué*' from texts treated as were the Hugo lines and the nursery songs in *Impressions d'Afrique*. We are given only two and a half lines of one such text, for a concluding episode. No clue is offered to anything in the substantial third or yet longer fourth chapter.

Canterel's guests are next led towards what appears to be a gigantic diamond, from which not only dazzling light but also music proceeds. It is in fact a many-faceted glass tank filled with a highly oxygenated, abnormally sparkling water, called *aqua micans*. Human beings and other terrestrial animals can breathe in it without difficulty, and the source of the music turns out to be the undulating hair of a well-known dancer, Faustine, who gracefully poses and sways there in pink fleshings. Rising and falling in the water are a number of ingeniously constructed Cartesian diving toys or bottle-imps, each illustrating a story. The tank also contains an entirely depilated Siamese cat and the brain, nervure and musculature of Danton's head, which, with the aid of a metal instrument concentrating its animal magnetism, the cat is able to galvanise into speech, lip-readable despite the head's fleshlessness. Seven sea-horses, normally kept in ordinary water nearby, are briefly placed in the *aqua micans*, where they have been trained to aquatic sports on which the visitors wager. In the Lake Ontario story, we have already come across one form of *séton*, a horse-doctor's device normally used to keep a cyst open and draining. It is a charming thought that even the tiny hippocampus may require veterinary treatment. To sport in the (to them) excessively oxygenated water, each of the seven trained sea-horses is enabled to discharge oxygen by means of a differently coloured exutory suture.

At the close of this third chapter, Faustine emerges from the tank and, still in her pink fleshings, accompanies the visitors, who, in the long fourth chapter, proceed to the paths surrounding a glass cage some fifty yards long. At eight points behind the glass (there is room in the cage for more) have been set up various stage-sets representing a ruined chapel in Italy, an unruined chapel in Brittany, the actual stage of a theatre, a sculptor's workshop and so on. In each of these settings, a scene, of which many of the details seem unintelligible, is re-enacted for the benefit of one or another small group of other visitors whom Canterel's guests have encountered on the paths surrounding the glass cage. In each scene, the protagonist is in fact a corpse, other figures being paid attendants, who are dressed in special underclothing against the intense cold. Repeatedly, for the consolation of his surviving loved ones, each of the dead re-enacts the most significant moments of his life, impelled thereto by the action upon his corpse of two substances, resurrectine and vitalium, developed by the learned and ingenious Canterel.

A preponderance of Roussel's stories elsewhere relate to periods remote in time, and sometimes they add apocryphal detail to the life of a real historical personage. In addition to Danton's head, a bottle-imp in the *aqua micans* had acted out a story of Wagner, while, as we have seen, Handel appeared in *Impressions d'Afrique*. By reason of the mere fact that they had to die after Canterel's discovery of means to factitious revivification, the stories connected with the scenes in the glass cage are of necessity near-contemporary and concern imaginary but credible Europeans. We might thus expect them to bring us closer than usual to the man Roussel's always elusive sense of reality. I do not find that they do this, except insofar as Roussel was an artist and as a number of the dead men were ingenious artists, at least one of them a suicide. What we do find, however, is something we might regard as a physical obverse of psycho-analysis. In the recovery of the mentally injured Seil Kor in *Impressions d'Afrique*, we got the restoration of a sense of reality through the reliving of past experience, theatrically represented. In the eight re-enactments in the long fourth chapter of *Locus Solus*, it is the beholders who are healed or consoled by the apparent reliving of a crucial experience, commonly of a traumatic nature. I do not know what, by 1914, Roussel had picked up about the essential nature of psycho-analytical therapy. Certainly, he was always much concerned with the restoration of a thing past, with something resembling Platonic recollection, Kierkegaardian repetition, with the *redintegratio in pristinum*.[1] And theatrical false-face, we may also think, seemed to him more, at once, of a traumatic and of a healing instrument than anything to be found in the hitherings and thitherings of daily life.

A *crise salutaire* is sought also in the fifth chapter. It is now twilight. The visitors move to a commodious cell opening on one side, by way of a large iron gate, on to the forest. Inside, a mad sculptor and inventor, believing himself to be Leonardo da Vinci, recapitulates the terrible scene in which he once saw his infant daughter trampled to death by drunken brigands in the wilds of Kent, dancing 'Sir Roger de Coverley' as a form of deliberately lethal exercise. The madman is on his way to recovery, partly through the recreation of his daughter's voice on a primitive form of acoustic phonograph.[2] A well-known British tune plays its part also in the longer and more elaborate sixth chapter, where tiny insects inserted with delicate watchmaker's mechanism inside the cards of a Tarot pack respond with curious effect to the singing of 'The Bluebells of Scotland'. This chapter also exhibits a gallinaceous bird of gorgeous plumage and strange tail-formation from Borneo. Both in this sixth and in the seventh and final chapter, fortune-tellers appear, and one of the

[1] In his youthful essay on Roussel, M. Butor brought out something of this in a comparison of Roussel with Proust, as one enthralled by the idea of time regained.

[2] We may note that Jules Verne's *Carpathian Castle* contains the ideas both of a preserved voice and of the hallucinatory revivification of a dead loved one. Roussel's debt to Jules Verne could hardly be over-estimated.

visitors is discountenanced. The star of the final chapter is a gallinaceous bird, the cock Mopsus.

It is an intelligent bird which, deprived of other means of expression, forms letters in its abnormally congested throat and then coughs them out in blood on to a tablet of ivory, by these means spelling out words and even composing prophetic alexandrines. Roussel in 1932 did not remember all the details, but he quotes lines from his own poem *La Source* (in his second volume, *La Vue*) and tells us what phonic association caused them to yield. From '*Elle commence tôt sa tournée asticote*' came '*Ailé coma . . . Saturne élastique hotte*' and thus a bird immobile as in a trance, communing with the planet Saturn and wearing on its back a receptacle like that worn by grape-harvesters but flexible. From '*Avec un parti pris de rudesse ses gens/Qui tous seraient*' we get '*Ave cote part type rit des rues (type des rues rit) d'essai sauge. En qui toux sert*'. The cock's master is a *type des rues*, and he laughs when Mopsus offers a flower of meadow sage to Faustine, who also murmurs an *Ave*. That coughing is made to serve the purposes of divination, we have seen. The suggestion of '*cote*' and '*part*' is somewhat general and vague, but we may see where Roussel has toyed with various senses of the former word, as betting odds, quota, dimensions, marks and letters, even perhaps as the quantum line in surveying (the rod focussed on Saturn through which Mopsus absorbs the planet's influence), while Faustine dreams of going away, giving up all for love and not counting the cost. From the separate word '*déluge*', Roussel also tells us, he formed '*dé l'eus-je?*' and so a dice and the questioning enigma printed on it in red and black, '*L'ai-je eu? l'ai-je? l'aurai-je?*' We are told that '*l'eus-je*' was changed to '*l'ai-je eu*' because Roussel feared that the close collocation of '*dé*' and '*l'eus-je*' might give his game away, the pun being exact phonetically.

The name of the young *type des rues* who turned out to be a genius at divination is Noël. He could have been (though he is not) described as a '*devin enfant*'. I owe to M. Brunius the immediately convincing suggestion that what lay verbally in the background here was the '*divin enfant*' of so many Christmas carols or *chansons de Noël*.

V

THE TWO PLAYS

IN THE ABSENCE of full texts and numerous photographs and drawings, it is difficult to imagine how certain things in *Impressions d'Afrique* and *Locus Solus* were ever presented on a stage. No doubt, in *Impressions d'Afrique*, something was done with gauze and lighting for Fogar's subaqueous adventures, but it must have been difficult to persuade the ladies of the ballet, liberally smeared with burnt cork, to perform a dance while belching repeatedly. In *Locus Solus*, was there a trained cock for Mopsus or a maltreated bird of paradise for the *iriselle* of the penultimate chapter? In both books, moreover, but more especially in *Locus Solus*, many of the marvels exhibited are on a finely microscopic scale and, however cleverly faked, would hardly be visible to a large audience. One of the photographs discovered and acquired by Mr. Ashbery and reproduced in *Bizarre* in 1964 does indeed show how (pages 56–9 of *Impressions of Africa*) Skariofszky's earthworm playing on a zither was displayed, though one cannot see the worm itself and does not know what it was made of, how it was activated and whether its presumed movements were such as to catch the eye of a man at the back of the stalls or in the upper circle. In camera close-up, we might even be clearly shown the musical insects set in the thickness of a Tarot card (in the sixth chapter of *Locus Solus*). On a screen, the bottle-imps (third chapter) would come up marvellously, and, if they could be managed, the agitated nervure of Danton's head and (even better) the racing sea-horses would be great delights. One wonders if MM. Robbe-Grillet and Alain Resnais ever toyed with the idea of filming *Impressions d'Afrique* or *Locus Solus*. Nobody, I feel sure, would ever think of staging either again.

In *L'Étoile au Front* and *La Poussière de Soleils*, written for theatrical performance in the first place, there is nothing either flatly impossible for the stage or likely to be unintelligible or invisible upon it. Indeed, with the more lightly stylised and fluid methods of presentation used today, it is not inconceivable that *La Poussière de Soleils* should make an agreeable evening's entertainment. No amount of ingenious stagecraft or subtlety of performance could preserve *L'Ètoile au Front* from the prompt onset of boredom and irritation in an audience, despite the many incidental splendours.

L'étoile au front was first performed at the Vaudeville on May 5th, 1924. The names of more than one actor in the original cast look vaguely familiar, and with one of them, by then a tremendously senior member of the Comédie Française, Jean Yonnel, I had, as it happens, to do professionally some twelve years ago, with much gratification (but at that time had not even heard the name of Raymond Roussel). The framework of the play is conventional. There are three acts. The first takes place in a drawing-room in Marly, the second in the grounds of the same house a week or more later and the third in an antique shop in Paris. The time is (or was) the present. The characters are a rich collector, two young people, betrothed to each other, who are in his tutelage, the antique dealer, his wife and son, a lawyer, a half-Indian female servant, a male Indian in love with her, another servant and two Indian twin girls who have been saved by the collector from a temple sacrifice. In the first act, it appears that there is to be a main plot, concerned with the abduction or murder of the twin girls by the male Indian, recently arrived in France, and at the end of the act some element of real drama appears in his playing on the divided loyalties of the half-

Indian servant. We might have been a little worried, during the act, by the marked disposition of the collector and the betrothed couple to tell each other stories about various *objets d'art* in the room and about the authors of books, but we might also have supposed that these would in due course find their place in the action. We should have noticed two oddities about the dialogue, in the first place the extreme *naïveté* of the many lines of the my-father-as-you-know-was-a-butcher type and in the second place the not always ineffective but soon irritating tendency the characters have to prompt each other with their stories, as though some old theatrical hand had told Roussel to break up his dialogue as much as possible and he had taken the advice excessively to heart.

Early in the second act, we learn that the Indian twins have been moved elsewhere for safety and that the male Indian and the half-Indian servant have gone away, and that is the last we hear of any of the four. The antique-dealer's appearance in the garden and, in the final act, the visits to the antique shop of the collector and the engaged couple and the lawyer merely provide occasions for the various characters to tell each other further stories. All these stories, we must presume from what we are told in *Comment J'Ai Écrit Certains de mes Livres*, were suggested by verbal procedures like those used for episodes in *Impressions d'Afrique* and *Locus Solus*. We are, however, given specific clues only to one, quite minor episode, that in Act II, Scene IV, of the pope St. Julius, where the word '*singulier*' gave us the name and '*pluriel*' the '*pelure*' in the sense of an outer garment (which, equally in English, one peels off) taken from the crib of Jesus to keep a child warm. In 1932, there existed among Roussel's papers a very full documentation for the two plays, but apparently this has not yet been turned up.

A number of the stories told on-stage concern, as do stories in all Roussel's large prose-works, real-life personages, here Milton, Rameau and Lope de Vega. The story of Lope de Vega is told in Act I, Scene III, by Geneviève to her *fiancé* Claude. This appealing story concerns a former mistress of Lope's who becomes abbess of a convent for penitent young female sinners. The tradition is that, before she takes the veil, a headless plaster cast is made of each nun's body, and the casts are disposed over a large terrace about a statue of Mary Magdalene, in token of all the desirable young flesh she has saved from perdition. In his later years and at the height of his fame, Lope visits the convent in an official capacity. He will see the plaster casts and know that one of them is that of his former mistress's body. She wishes discreetly to inform him which of them it is, so that his eye will not wander. This she achieves by causing the arrangement of flowers in a triumphal arch to cast on the place of her heart a horizontal figure eight, the mathematical sign for infinity, which a gipsy woman had once traced on the ground for them in answer to a question at the time of their love.

I find this haunting. I also believe (not without murmured assent from him) that it haunted M. Robbe-Grillet, who in *Le Voyeur* makes a very different but no less obsessive use of the horizontal figure eight. A further story in Act II of *L'Étoile au Front* is doubly concerned, as between a king and a queen in a play and as between the actor and actress playing them, with images of desirable nudity, in these two cases not retrospectively but prospectively important. *L'Étoile au Front* was the first work written after a presumed crisis which had taken Roussel to Janet and caused the latter to write about his patient. I do not want to make too much of these tenuous indications, but it is almost as though one were witnessing a timid rebirth of something resembling adult sexuality after twenty-five years of repression, for there was an element of sensuality in *La Doublure*, at the time of the first crisis, and there is none in any of the writing which intervenes.

Alas, the play as a play is lamentable. In real life, nothing is more tedious than the capping of one story by another, whether of dirty stories among members of the commercial classes or of intrinsically wittier anecdotes among people of more education and refinement. The play's reception by its first public was no mere exhibition of unreceptive philistinism. Nowhere perhaps does Raymond Roussel show powerful constructional, architectonic gifts, but at best, like Boccaccio, an artful grouping of his miniatures. In no other work, however, does over-all imagination seem to have deserted him so completely as in *L'Étoile au Front*, despite an original determination to arrange all within the framework of a conventional three-act play. Faced only with this work, one might, I feel, have concluded that Raymond Roussel was simply mad, with all that the idea implies in the way of mental incapacity, imaginative incoherency. He was forty-seven when the play was put on.

The title, it has already been pointed out, connects up with 'the brand on one's brow, the star one bears resplendent', in the Janet account. It is unconnected with anything whatever in the play until, at the last moment, it appears to provide a poetical flourish and a curtain line. We are referred to the work of a learned psychograph in which a spiritual and creative *élite* are described as having been born, though humbly and of obscure life, with a star on the forehead, a star presumably invisible to all but the spiritual eye. A valuable copy of this book is given by the antique dealer to Geneviève, who concludes the play by saying that perhaps her firstborn will have a star on its forehead.

La Poussière de Soleils, two years later, similarly ends on the words of its title, which are equally unrelated to all that has gone before. All the same, it is a better play. Roussel's odd verbal procedures in themselves are not unlike treasure-hunt clues, and the action of *Poussière* is a treasure hunt, the treasure being a real fortune, its bequeather the formulator of clues and the rival teams mortally in earnest. Here, too, stories are told on the stage, but they are told within relevant situations, and a degree of real suspense is maintained.

There are twenty-four scenes in the play, *tableaux* not *scènes*, i.e., they are scenes in the English sense, in that for each scene the stage must be newly set, not merely in the French classical sense, according to which the entrance or departure of a character marks a new scene. The twenty-four scenes are grouped in five acts, but the division is purely conventional, and a producer today would be likely to arrange that there should be one interval or two. There are not twenty-four distinct sets, since we revert twice to the first scene and twice to the third and once each to three other scenes. There are seventeen sets, and the original published edition, like that of today, contained a coloured picture of each by the authors of the settings, MM. Numa and Chazot.

The play was mounted at the Porte Saint-Martin on the 2nd of February, 1926. The stage had to be dressed twenty-four times for each performance, twenty-three during performance. As there were four intervals between acts, only nineteen of these changes had to be accomplished while the audience sat in its place and the orchestra played music, by a M. Marius-François Gaillard, which I hope Mr. Ashbery may be able to turn up for us one day. Unless this was particularly good, the best-mannered audience must have fidgeted, however devoted and skilful the scene-shifters were. The point, however, of dwelling upon the numbers of sets, scene-changes, scenes in the English sense, scenes (fifty in all) in the French sense, is to make certain that nowhere does the figure twenty-two come into it all. For André Breton, bent on proving that Raymond Roussel was an initiate of some occult religion, insists in his *Fronton Virage* essay that *La Poussière de Soleils* significantly contained twenty-two changes of scene, twenty-two being the number of *arcana* in the Tarot pack, as of letters in the Hebrew alphabet. If, in underpinning *Les Gommes* with obscure but demonstrable (demonstrated by Bruce Morrissette) references to the Tarot *arcana*, M. Robbe-Grillet was affected at all by *La Poussière de Soleils*, it cannot have been by Roussel's practice but only by M. Breton's eager adoption of a simple numerical mistake made in the first place by M. Ferry.

The time is again (or, forty years ago, was again) the present, the setting French Guiana. The legitimate heir, Julien Blache, has arrived to take up his uncle's inheritance. Apart from what is declared in the will, a hoard of jewels is supposed and finally proved to exist. It has been placed, as we learn in the last scene, down a well. The clues in general lead from a book or a picture to a person and back again to some other book or person. A group of local bad men are also after the treasure, but end up in prison.

A sub-plot concerns Blache's daughter and a young man with whom she falls in love. He is a foundling, but in due course establishes a glorious ancestry. An oddly contemporary note is struck when it transpires that he has been carrying a banner in a procession on behalf of the rights of negroes throughout the American continent. No more than anything else in his work does this mean that Roussel entertained 'liberal' views. Solange disapproves. So does an indisputably virtuous friend of her father's, who considers the demonstration at once foolish and disreputable. The young man himself forgets all about it. These counter-indications do not mean, on the other hand, that Roussel entertained 'reactionary' views. The political news and other people's notions about such matters were, I am sure, of purely objective concern to him.

I must here revert to the question of adult sexuality, to tenderness addressed otherwise than to little girls. In an early scene between the lovers, Jacques, the foundling, gives Solange a fine missal he has won in a lottery. In return, she takes out, from beneath her bodice, a locket she had once received as a prize at her convent. She gives him this, and he expresses tender delight at a gift warmed by her contact and for so long worn by her intimately, *i.e.*, between her breasts. This is conventional enough, but it is not the kind of thing one finds in *Impressions d'Afrique*, *Locus Solus* or the early stories. Also near the beginning of *Poussière*, recounting the mixed descent of a local female personality, one of Blache's allies tells him that her mother, a European dignitary's wife, organised some theatricals, during the course of which she was detected by her husband in the arms of a native who had been cast in the rôle of a coloured eunuch and who, at that moment, '*s'employait activement à lui prouver qu'il n'était pas du tout entré dans la peau de son personnage*'. It is a well-constructed, well-placed joke and, delivered with expert timing, must have been good for a laugh in any theatre. Nothing of the kind occurs elsewhere in Roussel.

As with *L'Étoile au Front*, the play's title is irrelevantly stuck on.

At the end of *La Poussière de Soleils*, Jacques must go away briefly before he and Solange are married. During their separation, Solange suggests that each shall contemplate a particular star in the heavens at night. Jacques, on the other hand, recommends that they shall gaze at the Milky Way, which, he explains, is a positive dust-cloud of suns, each bigger than ours.

VI

THE *NOUVELLES IMPRESSIONS*

Nouvelles Impressions D'Afrique was begun in 1915 and finished in 1928. It is a poem in four cantos or *chants*, totalling twelve hundred and seventy-six lines. The final version, apparently, took seven years to write, five years having previously been 'wasted' on a version differently conceived (stated, in 1932, still to have been preserved among Roussel's papers). If *Impressions d'Afrique* is not quite the travel book its title would suggest, it is at least set in an imaginary Africa, and a large number of its characters are to be understood to be negroes. The *Nouvelles Impressions* hardly mention Africa or anything supposedly African, though each canto is given the title of a tourist attraction in Egypt and opens with a brief reflection upon it.

A highly skilled poet or verse-craftsman might, I suppose, one day assiduously produce a translation, in regular, rhymed verse, of the *Nouvelles Impressions d'Afrique*. It would be a hard and perhaps a thankless task, and no near future seems likely to confront the reader with a *Further Impressions of Africa* in English. I must therefore describe the poem as well as I can. Having committed myself to the view that *Impressions d'Afrique* is Roussel's masterpiece, I am left without a convenient term for 'placing' the *Nouvelles Impressions*, but, among works all in their own way unique (the plays perhaps least so), this is in some way a peak or summit, as the mere difficulty of scaling it demonstrates.

I cannot, I fancy, more usefully begin than by simply showing the reader how the poem looks upon the page. Thus, for example, near the beginning of the first canto, we read:

> Le nom dont, écrasé, le porteur est si fier
> Que de mémoire, à fond, il sait sans une faute
> (Comme sait l'occupant, dans une maison haute,
> D'un clair logis donnant sur le dernier palier
> —Photographe quelconque habile à pallier
> Pattes d'oie et boutons par de fins stratagèmes—
> ((Pouvoir du retoucheur! lorsque arborant ses gemmes
> (((Chacun, quand de son moi, dont il est entiché,
> Rigide, il fait tirer un orgueilleux cliché,
> —Se demandant, pour peu qu'en respirant il bouge,
> Si sur la gélatine, à la lumière rouge,
> Dans le révélateur il apparaîtra flou,—
> ((((Tels se demandent:—S'il diffère d'un filou,
> Le fat qui d'un regard (((((parfois une étincelle,
> L'entourant de pompiers qui grimpent à l'échelle,
> Fait d'un paisible immeuble un cratère qui bout[1]:)))))
> Enflamma, dépourvu lui de toute fortune. . . .

> [1] Que n'a-t-on, lorsqu'il faut d'un feu venir à bout,
>   Un géant bon coureur,—quand une maison flambe,
>   Un sauveteur loyal doit-il traînant la jambe,
>   Considérer de loin la besogne en boudeur?—
>   Qui, prêt, tel Gulliver, à vaincre sa pudeur,
>   Aurait à satisfaire une envie opportune.

Each canto is allowed to go up to five pairs of brackets more than once. The passage above, for instance, goes on for several pages within the four brackets within which we may consider ourselves to be standing when the quotation ends, then goes again briefly into five before progressively easing into three, two, one and finally no brackets. Parentheses between dashes may occur within any set of brackets, while the footnotes in verse are in effect sixth pairs of brackets. They are closely integrated into the general structure. It will be noted, for instance, that, in the quotation above, it is the first line of the footnote which takes up the rhyme, while its last line rhymes with the first line of what then follows in the body of the text. In this same canto, there is a line which breaks off at the caesura, referring us to a footnote which, metrically speaking, though not in sense, completes the line and of course bears the rhyme. In the fourth canto, the lines in footnote are more numerous than those in the body of the text.

These are distressing and rebarbative typographical oddities. Afterthoughts had never been allowed so to proliferate within a printed text. The very idea of parenthesis seems here to have been reduced to absurdity. The poem is indeed 'unreadable' in any usual and consecutive manner. J. B. Brunius devised a 'machine for reading Roussel' which was exhibited at the big *surréaliste* exhibition in 1938. This was a table on a tripod, about which the reader was required to walk. Others, since, have constructed things with handles. The idea was in all cases to make it possible quickly to by-pass brackets. Roussel himself had apparently toyed with the idea not of multiplied brackets but of differently coloured printers' inks (I am no printer, but I can see what difficulty and expense would have been involved). As M. Brunius has also shown, certain aids to reading were envisaged by Roussel in the original presentation of his text or, at any rate, the avoidance of certain obstacles to reading. The important thing was not to cut the pages.

For Roussel had decided, in the first place, that the volume would be too slim. He almost quadrupled its thickness by, first, commissioning a fixed number of whole-page illustrations and, second, by having nothing printed on left-hand pages, so that, with the *Nouvelles Impressions* proper (it may be recalled that the book also contains *L'Âme de Victor Hugo*), the text appears on only one page in four (with *L'Âme de Victor Hugo* on one page in two, but with a wide space between pairs of stanzas, the rhyme-pattern meaningfulness of which is lost in the current Pauvert edition). The crude illustrations, by one H.-A. Zo, were commissioned through a private detective agency, and the artist was sent written instructions. The book was so printed that you could read the whole text without cutting the pages and need not then see the illustrations at all. The precise instructions sent to Zo (and, one must say, conscientiously and intelligently fulfilled by him) result at one point in the drawing of a man peering curiously between uncut pages.

Certainly, once its pages are cut, a copy of the old Lemerre edition becomes almost unmanageable. In the new Pauvert edition, the illustrations, reduced in size, are printed all together at the end of the poem, and, as there are more lines on a page, the amount of leafing backwards and forwards is reduced. It is not obviated. There is no real way of obviating it. A machine does not obviate it, really. M. Ferry's way, in *Une Ètude sur Raymond Roussel*, of printing a whole canto on one large, folded sheet merely substitutes other and possibly greater difficulties. A reader's approach to each of the four cantos is bound to follow what must have been the order of its composition, unless the reader enjoys a capacity for bracketing things off successively in his memory which I imagine to be characteristic only of a handful of chess-players, mathematicians and philosophers in any generation. The odd thing is that in detail the poem presents few difficulties, even to a foreigner. Its vocabulary, for instance, is small, compared with that of *Impressions d'Afrique* or *Locus Solus*, and contains no large number of words which may be taken in two or more senses.

The four cantos take their points of departure from, respectively, a house at Damietta in which the sainted Louis IX of France was imprisoned after his first crusade, the scene of the Napoleonic battle of the Pyramids, a mosque near Damietta, where, it appears, one could be cured of jaundice by licking a stone until one's tongue bled, and the gardens at Rosetta. Roussel had travelled in Egypt, but we know his distaste for making use of real observation. The abortive version of the *Nouvelles Impressions* had begun with images, one of bazaars in Cairo, one of the banks of the Nile at Luxor, found as photographs on glass in a minute pair of opera glasses worn as a pendant, each lens no more than two millimetres in diameter. The original poem would thus have been, in part, extrapolatorily descriptive, like the three poems which make up the volume *La Vue*. As starting points for the four cantos of the *Nouvelles Impressions*, we may imagine picture-postcards or what we will.

The capsule, as it were, of the first canto may be loosely translated as follows, a gap in the lines being left where interpolation subsequently takes place.

> No doubt it inclines one to reflect, to make calculations,
> When one is told that there, behind that door,
> The saintly king, Louis IX, was for three months a prisoner. . . .
> And yet how new, how tangible, the fact seems
> In this country where ruined marvels litter the ground,
> As old as any to be found in the world!
> In their presence, everything seems to date from yesterday:
> The name its ruined bearer is so proud of
> He knows by memory, without a mistake, through and through
>
> —Root, stem and branch, with the collateral branches—
> His ancestors' estate; defaced cathedrals;
> Even proud menhir, aboriginal cromlech,
> Dolmen beneath which the soil is always dry.

A pleasant enough little poem in itself, one line short of a sonnet and in manner not unlike the sonnets of Mallarmé. After the ninth line, however, Roussel took up the idea of familiarity and began comparing the destitute bearer of a great name with a man living on the top floor of a tall house, falling into a parenthesis between dashes before opening his second pair of brackets, as the reader may see from the page shown as a specimen some little way back. The comparison with a top-floor tenant is abandoned for a hundred and thirty lines, during which further analogies, explanations and lists of examples accumulate, and is completed in one line, the last bracket then being closed, immediately before the tenth line in the translated quotation above leads us to the end of the canto.

The very inmost of such a system of Chinese boxes would, of

course, be a parenthesis between dashes in a footnote to something already within five pairs of brackets. This may indeed be found on the specimen page in the figure of a hypothetically reluctant fireman. That tiny nucleus[1] may with some confidence be thought to be the last detail added by the author and ought to be the final point reached by the reader, who should go backward and forward, as it were peeling off the brackets pair by pair.

M. Ferry, *né* Jean Lévy, is best known in this country and perhaps in France for a single, magnificent short story, *Le Tigre Mondain*, which appears in Breton's *Anthologie de l'Humour Noir*, appeared in translation, as 'The Fashionable Tiger', in *The London Magazine* and has since reappeared, the translation perfected, in a Penguin collection of modern French short stories. M. Ferry has written other stories, even shorter, but is not a prolific writer. He has, however, devoted more years of his life to taking the *Nouvelles Impressions* to pieces than Raymond Roussel spent in putting them together.

The main fruit of this labour is *Une Étude sur Raymond Roussel*, published in 1953, a book almost wholly devoted to a line-by-line analysis of the second canto of *Nouvelles Impressions d'Afrique*. In the fascinating issue of *Bizarre* already mentioned, there are analyses of the first, third and fourth cantos. The analyses are much shorter, but so are the cantos. The second canto contains, with its rhymed footnotes, six hundred and forty-four lines, while, of the other three, the longest, which is the fourth canto, contains only two hundred and thirty-two lines, a hundred and thirty-four of which are in footnote.

What M. Ferry has done might have been done by another. If nobody had published the results of such a labour, the close student of Roussel would have had to do it for himself. It would be madness now for anybody to forego M. Ferry's help, especially with regard to the second canto.

[1] Nucleus only in a formal sense. It is really the final afterthought. The nucleus of the canto in a meaningful sense lies, formally, on the outside.

The point of departure is, it may be recalled, Napoleon's battle of the Pyramids, during his rather pointless Egyptian campaign. We may note that there are already two parentheses between dashes within the four lines which precede the opening of the first brackets and that when, six hundred lines later, these brackets are closed, we are still parenthetically engaged until the penultimate line, so that syntactically the whole canto is enclosed by its first line and by two lines at the end, which together state that merely to evoke the figure of Napoleon on this battlefield causes one to fall into meditation and forget Egypt, its sun, its evenings, its sky.

Within single brackets we get no more than six lines before double brackets open and two after they close, with a brief further single-bracket enclosure. Totally enclosed within double brackets, the arrangement becomes more complex than in the first canto, and the number of lines running unbrokenly between one moment of parenthetisation and the next is variable in the extreme. Mr. Ferry is fond of these little schematic diagrams, but seems not to have thought of this one, showing the distribution of numbers of lines, from l. II, when double brackets open, to l. 602, when they close.

$$(\, (\, 9 \, \text{ll.} \, (\, (\, (\, 2 \, \text{ll.} \,) \,) \,) \, 1\tfrac{1}{2} \, \text{ll.} \, (\, (\, (\, 4\tfrac{1}{2} \, \text{ll.} \,) \,) \,) \, 3\tfrac{1}{2} \, \text{ll.} \, (\, (\, (\, \tfrac{1}{2} \, \text{l.}$$
$$(\, (\, (\, (\, 3 \, \text{ll.} \,) \,) \,) \,) \, 3 \, \text{l.} \, (\, (\, (\, (\, 1 \, \text{l.} \, (\, (\, (\, (\, (\, 4 \, \text{ll.} \,) \,) \,) \,) \,) \, 1 \, \text{l.}$$
$$(\, (\, (\, (\, (\, 2 \, \text{ll.} \,) \,) \,) \,) \,) \, 2 \, \text{ll.} \, (\, (\, (\, (\, (\, 41 \, \text{ll.} \,) \,) \,) \,) \, 418 \, \text{ll.} \,) \,) \,) \,)$$
$$2 \, \text{ll.} \, (\, (\, (\, (\, 32 \, \text{ll.} \,) \,) \,) \,) \, 61 \, \text{ll.} \,) \,) \,) \, 1 \, \text{l.} \,) \,).$$

From this it may be seen that the second canto goes into five pairs of brackets three times and on one occasion stays there for more than forty lines, but that the greatest number of lines occurs within four pairs of brackets and the second-longest unbroken run within three. There are, of course, also the lines in footnote, but these are less numerous in this longest second canto than in any of the other three.

M. Ferry devotes a chapter each to the four longest series of lines consecutive in sense. These are catalogues, respectively, of things which diminish, of great things confounded with small ones, of the caprices of fortune and of foolish assertions or denials.

A man plays down his own faults. A shadow cast by the sun grows shorter towards noon. The standard metre in platinum shrinks in cold weather. A man rolls up his trousers to keep them out of the muck. There is a reference to the Romeo and Juliet performance in the gala performance of *Impressions d'Afrique*. And there are, both in this canto and elsewhere, as M. Ferry unhappily points out, rather numerous coprological references (one of the things which progressively diminishes is the paper in a lavatory). As M. Ferry also more happily says, this is the only work by Roussel in which there are signs of any such preoccupation. I don't think myself that they indicate obsession on a clinical scale. A lonely man may take longer to abandon schoolboy humour, and I would say that there is a good deal less coprophily in Roussel than, for instance, in James Joyce. I am sure that he felt lightly humorous about it all. Moreover, if you are cataloguing the daily phenomena of human life, we might argue that it is odder to leave all that side of things out than to include it.

The second series is by far the longest, and I do not propose to follow it out, either from the poem itself or from M. Ferry's contracted sequence (he does not deal with lines whose meaning and relevance are obvious, unless they suggest interesting reference elsewhere in Roussel's work, markedly the case with ll. 105–7, whose meaning M. Ferry says that he puzzled over for ten years before finally attaching it to the paviour's beetle in *Locus Solus*). The whole sequence is a curious *tour de force*, employing, as M. Ferry calculates, two hundred and six comparisons, most of them extravagant, between four hundred and twelve component elements selected one knows not how. As examples of what M. Ferry classifies (with perfect justice) as cases of the great confounded with the small, I select, as typically image-creating, the confusions of an adjustable spanner with a semiquaver rest, a photographer's tripod with the rejected stalks of a bunch of three cherries, a chamois horn with an eyelash, a stalactite in a cave with the uvula in a throat opened wide for inspection.

The capricious turning of fortune's wheel is illustrated by ruined businessmen, anxious heirs, Cinderella, Samson, Turenne, the drunkard, the prodigal son, Daniel in the lions' den, the pawn in a game of chess which, reaching the opponent's back line, may be changed for a queen, and so on. The catalogue of foolish asseverations is calculated to tax the urbanity of mine host, who, whatever a guest or customer says, must not contradict or even raise his eyebrows. I agree with M. Ferry that it is not a good list. Roussel lacked that kind of satirical ear for opinions.

One of the less decorous items may seem of interest to readers of Proust, who may have felt mildly puzzled when they read, on pages 163–4, in the first volume of the Scott-Moncrieff *Swann's Way:*

> What fascinated me would be the asparagus, tinged with ultramarine and rosy pink, . . . that precious quality which I should recognise again when, all night long after a dinner at which I had partaken of [asparagus heads], they played (lyrical and coarse in their jesting as the fairies in Shakespeare's *Dream*) at transforming my humble chamber into a bower of aromatic perfume.

The great translator has funked it. What the asparagus transformed was Marcel's chamber-*pot* (not described as humble) into a *vase* of perfume. One of the absurdities at which the ideal host must not bat an eyelid would be the denial that eating asparagus produces scented urine, at which the sated epicure will sniff with delight. The notion, as M. Ferry points out, has occurred already in the first canto, where the scented jet is directed against a tree, no doubt after a picnic. Marcel, it may be remembered, has earlier described his family as eating asparagus in quite unusual quantity that year.

The Mosque at Damietta, in which there stands a column which, if you lick it until your tongue bleeds, will cure you of jaundice, prompted Raymond Roussel simply to reflect, in five lines at the beginning and one at the end of his third canto, that it is certainly a drastic treatment to go wearing this stone away after thousands of other fools, but that there is no limit to what people will do in the hope of being cured.

This canto, too, has its system of brackets, but it is easier to read through consecutively than the others. The subject throughout is hope, hope which sends people to America (where they may try this or that way of making a fortune), deceiving hope, ways of giving rise to false expectations (various kinds of writing, including dud cheques), the disappointments of snobbery, disappointed writers. We are soon out of Egypt, but never far away from the subject of hope.

The fourth canto is the most obviously poetic, at any rate if we ignore the footnotes (which themselves, the reader may care to be informed, began in the previous canto to develop rudimentary bracket-systems of their own). I shall ignore the footnotes, but otherwise present this shortest canto rather more fully than those which precede it. It starts with a view of the gardens at Rosetta, as seen from a dahabeah, which is a Nile boat. The enclosing lines, *i.e.*, those innocent of all brackets, number only three at the beginning and one at the end, but they are quite directly evocative. They suggest, moreover, that Raymond Roussel may, for once, have made an exception to his rule and introduced something experienced on his travels and recalled.

> Skimming the Nile, I see fleeting-by two banks thick
> With flowers, wings, lightnings, rich green plants
> Of which a single one might furnish twenty of our drawing-rooms
>
> With foliage and glinting light and fruits.

First brackets open at the mention of drawing-rooms, pleasant rooms in which, at every departure, rumour is rife about the one who has just gone.

But this piece of social observation is interrupted at once by double brackets and goes uncompleted until the penultimate line, what interrupts it (to be itself at once interrupted) being in the first place a specific instance of a man leaving such a room in disgrace, whose own situation remains uncertain until the two antepenultimate lines. Simply describing *Nouvelles Impressions d'Afrique* for the benefit of readers who may never see the whole poem either in translation or in the original, perhaps at this point I may be allowed to start again and set out, in loose translation, those nine lines of the canto which lie outside three pairs of brackets, schematically representing the glancing backward and forward between three and five pairs meanwhile, it being understood that what I show as a quarter or three quarters of a line means only that it is markedly less or more than a half.

Skimming the Nile, I see fleeting-by two banks thick
With flowers, wings, lightnings, rich green plants
Of which a single one might furnish twenty of our drawing-rooms
(Gentle drawing-rooms where as soon as anyone has turned on his heel
    and gone
((Amusing themselves either with his cowardliness
(((3 ll.)))
And whether—made to be publicly gibed at and disgraced—
(((7¼ ll. ((((5¾ ll.))))) 1¼ ll. ((((11¾ ll. (((((2¾
ll.))))) 16¾ ll. (((((1½ ll.))))) 1½ ll. (((((1½
ll.))))) ¼ l. (((((¾ l.))))) 10 ll. (((((11 ll.))))) 1 l.
(((((3½ ll.))))) 5½ ll.)))) 3 ll.)))
He will only be able to turn the other cheek to those who have slapped
    him in the face,
Or with his rare gift for cheating at cards;))
Gossip breaks out about the one who has gone;)
With foliage and glinting light and fruits.

Three pairs of brackets had first briefly opened with a reflection on the tendency not to hit back. They open again to reflect on the rapidity with which the shorn lamb accustoms itself to the cold, the parrot to its chain and perch, the envious man to other people's success, the astronomer to starry wastes, a dumb man to writing on a slate. But this sequence is again broken at the mention of the envious man (to describe his sleepless nights) and again at the astronomer, concerning whom we have to wait until near the end before we hear anything definite, the rest of the canto alternating between four and five pairs of brackets. I now further venture upon a broad account of these sixty-seven and three quarters lines in an uneven pendulum swing, which the unwary reader may yet contrive to follow.

... A particular star appears today
Like a fire whose light compels us to blink
Which, when the waters covered, of the terrestrial rind,
All but the peaks which men had yet to climb,
Was already to be listed among dead worlds ...
—All fires go out, in ourselves as in nature;
On those packets we shall have to sign for
With a breath the sender blows out the seals in turn;
Age puts out certain fires; tireless, the cockerel
Takes pullet, ripe hen, dowager bird, all ...
The old cock chooses; cowards, in the rear,
Feel a heat which does not outlast danger
(((((Illusory fire, it yet burns; none, cleaning up,
Ever thought much of its ashes, nor did the hare[1]
See it make the frogs jump;))))); fever
Starts a fire which goes out when the man dies
Or when, so much taller sometimes as to threaten,
O chandeliers, your lower bulbs and crystals,
—Fever makes even adults grow, that is well-known—
By degrees he comes to cool convalescence,
Goaded by hunger eats enough for a hundred
And once more bears a fresh and ruddy tongue;
The fire which patiently melts a candle down
Goes out:—while falls the hammer when you sell
Furniture at an auction;—assailed by the wind,
When, by torchlight, a king is brought forth from his abode
With pomp which the heir, who prays for his death,

[1] The reference is to a La Fontaine fable. The hare, a symbol of cowardice, nevertheless, when it runs from imaginary danger, frightens a group of frogs in its passage. The expression 'avoir le fev au derrière' is idiomatic for being in a hurry.

Smoulders darkly to see attending him;
—When, brutal, from the mouth of a distant pistol,
Held by a champion whose every shot is a bull,
The lucky projectile severs wick or button;
—When a reader, in bed (((((back raised from the pillow,
Head in hand, his interest quickening like that))))),
Has just started some affecting passage
In which, a mother without ring (((((whom the world thinks chaste.
So thoroughly was the birth kept secret)))))
To whom (((((ready to join his affluent destiny with hers))))
An upper-crust banker has lost his heart for life,
A little shopgirl, a year after her fall,
Prepares her infant for a furtive christening
Which will not load a single comfit-dish,
If, for a joke, someone put in the candlestick
A trick-candle undetectably made
To burn only a short way down from the top;
—When, directed that way, a sudden sneeze
Is followed by the suggestion that God bless
The person whose nose it was; the sacred fire of genius
(((((Which so inflames the vanity of its chosen
He finds real stars in the sky above pitiable
In comparison with the new star on his forehead
And dreams of becoming the master caricatured
By all whose pencils are engaged in that task,
—An art born, it is said, one evening, from the mad profile on the wall
Offered to laughter by the victim's shadow—
At whose doorbell countless journalists ring,
Decorated with one of the twenty great ribbons,
He who often now goes to bed fasting
Like a believer swallowing the host)))))
Goes out when its possessor drivels with age
(((((A fire which, great though name or pseudonym,
In none is acknowledged unanimously;
—A man unlike a doll in a bazaar
Is not marked with his price;))))); on the wall, Belshazzar
Saw, in characters defying india-rubber or scraper,
Three words of fire shine . . . then go out; in man,

> The light of the eye goes out as tooth by tooth
> And hair by hair, without accident or shock,
> By the action of time alone, his head is disburdened. . . .

The astronomer accustomed to his starry wastes and the dumb man to his slate then briefly link us to the concluding lines translated earlier. And then, of course, there are the lines in footnote, which, as has been said, are more numerous than those in the body of the canto.

VII

FLIO AND THE SIX DOCUMENTS

In *Comment J'Ai Écrit Certains de mes Livres*, Roussel tells us that, in addition to the earlier works he there included, there exists among his papers an episode notably concerned with Voltaire and a site full of *lucioles*, that is to say of glow-worms and/or fire-flies. It was written immediately after *Locus Solus* and interrupted by the mobilisation of 1914, but, says Roussel, it would perhaps be worth publishing one day, and so no doubt it was very nearly completed and would stand as it is. This manuscript has never come to light. At least, neither it nor any rumour of it has so far come the way of the present writer.

A typescript, markedly incomplete, of the same period was published in *Bizarre*, briefly introduced by Michel Leiris, with whose father, Eugène Leiris, it had been deposited on December 10th, 1914, Roussel having apparently by then been called up for military service. *Flio* may not have been its intended title. The word is in small letters, followed by the page-number 1, and M. Ferry's suggestion is that it should have been *Folio*. The typescript is full of slips and misspellings, and M. Ferry makes out a good case for supposing that it was typed back from dictation by a stenographer (we may care to remind ourselves that 1914 was the year in which, with the British 'Royal', that admirable invention the typewriter, a machine which must certainly have pleased Raymond Roussel, became standardised in the form from which it has never since departed in any essential). It is, in any case, very much a first draft, and it is fascinating to see how names are changed, things set down for earlier insertion and, about half way through, a radical modification introduced which would have involved fundamentally reshaping the first pages.

All stems from the island of B., off the south-west coast of Africa. Outside every hut are two groups of statuary, one depicting virtuous toil, the other unbridled licentiousness. These commemorate two phases in B . . . ian history, one during which the people so gave themselves up to the pleasures of love that the economy collapsed and one during which, recalled to order, they proceeded to the opposite extreme, the men castrating themselves so that they should not be diverted from work, with the result that the population almost died out. The two kinds of statuary are to remind the B . . . ians that a salutary balance must be preserved.

In the first pages of Roussel's draft, it is a young man, R., at first said to be a nobly born poet and sculptor and then a poet, the son of a sculptor, who visits B. and subsequently publishes two volumes of poems, one about the statues '*pourvus de pagnes*' and the other about those '*dépourvus de pagnes*' or, as we might say, those with girt and those with ungirt loins. These poems are closely descriptive, and some of those describing the ungirt statuary are thus of an extreme indelicacy. At first we are told that copies of the two volumes came into the hands of the widowed bibliophile, Cros . . . , Crosmel or Crosinel, whose story is then partly told. Presently, however, Roussel decided that Cros must himself be the author of the poems.

Cros has an adored but pathetically feeble-minded daughter, E. His already widowed sister dies, leaving a son, at first called Silvio, then called Han and said to be (presumably on his father's side only) Dutch, apparently because he is to be drowned while skating (Dutchmen notoriously skate) and perhaps also to bring him closer to the Scandinavian legend with which E. has identified him, where-upon a second brother-in-law of Cros appears, a Dutch sailor, who procures the requisite white bear.

77

For the prince in the legend, with whom E. had identified her adored Han, had been transformed into a white bear, and by persuading her that Han has been so transformed temporarily Cros hopes and contrives to stay his daughter's grief. The name of Madame d'Aulnoy placed here in brackets no doubt indicates some parallel with the white cat in one of her stories.

The licentious poems have gone out of print, and a new edition is required. Cros decides that it shall be made up of ten small volumes, graded as to licentiousness and, to this end, discreetly ornamented with screens or filtering web designs of varying mesh. A story is told to account for this procedure. The volume in which Cros has been grading the poems in this way is replaced, by a servant, to the wrong side of the poems '*pourvus de pagnes*' on Cros's meticulously ordered shelves.

On the evening of the fatal day, which, it appears, is also the anniversary of Han's drowning. . . . And here the narrative ends. M. Ferry considers that what is to make the day fatal is that the worst obscenities shall by mistake be read by E., a view to which we may reasonably be led by the extreme care with which the misplacing of the two volumes, externally indistinguishable, is described. No doubt the white bear might also have had its part to play. But no doubt also we shall never know.

That a feeble-minded girl shall die as the result of encountering obscenity on the anniversary of her betrothed's death, represented to her as his transformation into a white bear, might be made to carry all kinds of psychological overtones. Han and E. were first cousins. Germaine and Raymond Roussel were brother and sister. M. Ferry suggests that the word '*fin*' has got itself on to the last page of a clearly unfinished typescript because Roussel was unwilling to dictate the end of these troubled matters to a doubtless female stenographer. He may, at least, have felt out of his depth. Certainly, when he took up writing again the following year, it was not to this story he returned, but to a first version of what were to be the *Nouvelles Impressions*. It may be regretted.

There is a story within a story in *Flio*. Stories within stories are characteristic of all Roussel's work in prose. Nowhere else, however, is this tendancy taken to such extremes as in the six *Documents Pour Servir de Canevas*. These have not been authoritatively dated, but it seems likely enough that they were composed between 1928, when the *Nouvelles Impressions* were completed, and 1932, when Raymond Roussel began to put his posthumous work together. There were, a Lemerre note tells us, to have been thirty of these documents in all, and a prefatory episode in Cuba wa first suppressed, then destroyed, on Roussel's instructions.

M. Ferry supposes that each of the documents would have been considerably expanded, and certainly to describe them as serving the purpose of so many canvases suggests that some elaboration was to take place upon them. On the other hand, their narrative pace is not, for the most part, appreciably different from that which is common in the prose works, and thirty documents of the length of all but the shortest of these would have made up a sizeable book without expansion.

Story interrupts story as the matter within further brackets constantly interrupts the course of the thought in *Nouvelles Impressions d'Afrique*, so that in consecutive reading one has in general forgotten, by the time one reaches the end and briefly returns to it, what the initial story was about. In the first document, for example, when we have followed Romé's religious career, the history (connected with Mary Magdalene again) of the Grey Cross order he joins, learnt of the downfall of Fircine and how Romé consoled her with a story of Cacitaine, a Galilean in Jesus's time, and of the story within a story told them by the learned hermit Danecteur and that Romé was killed, it comes as a shock when Fircine takes a posy of faded campanulas, tied with a golden hair, back to a young woman called Eda and, looking back, we remember that it all began with this young woman being driven from her grandmother's cottage by the wicked Sire de Courty, round about 1485, in Burgundy, because she would not yield to his base desires. Ah, yes, we recall, Romé had seen her sleeping in the forest, had fallen in love with her, so that he could never love another, and yet had dared neither to wake her then nor to seek her out later, fearing lest her eyes might be less beautiful than the rest of her person.

The second document opens at a later date, in 1880, at St. Nazaire, where a poet of sea and sailors, Pérot or Pérou, dies a few days after his hundredth birthday, on which he danced a sailor's dance and after which he wrote all but the last line of a sonnet about himself, thereafter carved on a statue erected to him. Here, helpfully, a white line is drawn across the page. We next hear of a man who gains a great fortune by following a succession of three 'unlucky' indications provided by his late father, an ardent member of the Anti-Superstition League. These link us with St. Nazaire and Pérou, in that the clues provided by a broken mirror direct the intended heir to the statue with thirteen lines and thence along a line towards Friday, a rock out at sea (one of a pair, called Robinson and Friday). The fact is reported in the papers by the Anti-Superstition League and there read by one Claude Migrel who, at the end of the document, hopes to cure with it a son who has gone out of his mind on hearing of a dreadful crime taking place on a Friday the thirteenth. Between these two points, we are concerned with the reasons for the illiteracy of Migrel's son, with a statue in black and red marble near Marengo, commissioned by Napoleon from a sculptor whose own story we learn, then with the story behind the crime, itself complicated by events as remote in time as 1388 and as far away as Mexico and Sweden. We may read on with a sense that each of these numerous matters is naturally associated with that which preceded and that which is to follow it. Anyone reaching the end of a first reading might safely be offered a substantial prize if he could then reconstruct in his mind the pattern of the whole or any substantial proportion of the associative links. Yet the document in its entirety occupies less than ten pages in the current edition of *Comment J'Ai*, thirteen in the original Lemerre edition.

In the third document, we encounter no such complexities. In a chapel at Lourdes, a young girl reads aloud two pieces dictated by St. Bernadette, one the edifying account of a dream of fairyland, the other a cradle song for the infant Jesus (we are not given this), then shows two relics, a bone and a branch, and tells the stories connected with them, the stories of two small miracles performed by Bernadette, in one case restoring a thumb which a conscript had cut off to avoid military service, in the other saving a man from drowning by giving him directions which he will find have saved him from a dangerous patch of thin ice. And that is all.

The fourth document tells a variety of stories, but these are not folded inside each other in such a way as to confuse the reader's mind. We may, it is true, afterwards turn back and wonder why an account of the eight scenes of a quasi-historical play should be preceded by an explanation not only of how its author became famous and had the play put on but also of how the ambassador of Honduras in Paris came to be recalled to his native land, to the delight of his son, who admires the author of the play. Neither ambassador nor son reappears at the end, nor do the dice responsible for the poet's fame. The play itself is distinct from all the rest. Each scene has its own story, like the scenes in *La Poussière de Soleils*, whose setting, it may be remembered, had lain in the same general direction as Honduras.

In form, the fifth document is even more remarkably serial. No fewer than twenty wholly separate matters are meditated when Armand Vage passes a card, in which are two slits, over the pages of a book put together with scissors and paste by his miserly sister, recently deceased. On the twenty-first page, he finds the clue to her treasure, buried in the garden. He bequeathes it to the infantry regiment of which he was senior officer, having years ago surprised his wife *en galant duo* and clubbed her to death. His anniversary is kept in the regiment, falls into desuetude and is revived. These facts have no connection with the twenty little stories on the pages which did not furnish the clue.

Equally disconnected from the occasion on which he sings them are the subjects of the seventeen patter-songs sung by a Belotinian tenor, Furdot, to keep up the spirits of the dictator's troops during a siege, in the sixth document. Nor are they connected with the story of the revolution which had left the dictator in power, a lowborn man who has, however, put himself to school for manners to an aristocrat whose story also is told.

That word-pairing and the *procédé évolué* lie behind both *Flio* and these later pieces must, I fancy, be evident from the mere feel of them to anyone mildly saturated in Roussel's prose. That is perhaps not a very satisfactory way of putting it. Neither a critic nor a mere critics' guide ought to depend very much on intuition. All I can really offer in the way of evidence is that both *Flio* and the later pieces, but especially these, show more in the way of odd collocations of word and idea than would seem likely ever to arise naturally in the strangest imagination. At the same time, I am somewhat convinced (again, I'm afraid, by 'the mere feel') that, particularly in *Flio* and in the earlier of the six documents, the procedures themselves were less effortful and more lightly invoked, that the free imagination was allowed more scope. The mind of Raymond Roussel had evolved an extraordinary capacity for generating stories. Contrariwise, towards the end of the six documents, I feel, on the one hand, that the facility is getting out of hand and, on the other, that the procedures are being worked hard and that they are being used as brakes, which is not at all the purpose they were designed for.

If we must distrust intuition, we should perhaps distrust it especially when informed hindsight also is brought in. We know that a breakdown took place. As to writing, '*C'est tellement difficile!*' was what Roussel said to M. Leiris at the beginning of 1933. Certainly, I find the six *Documents Pour Servir de Canevas* unrewarding and am inclined to think that towards the end of them we might have guessed at some deterioration of mind and predicted that the work would never be finished.

VIII

FURTHER CONSIDERATIONS

THOSE ATTRACTED by the writings of Raymond Roussel have from the beginning found it difficult to say with any precision what it was they found there. To the *surréalistes* he early became, with Lautréamont, the greatest '*magnétiseur*' (the expression is that of their spokesman, André Breton) of our time. This need mean nothing more than that Lautréamont and Roussel, among their predecessors, specially attracted the *surréalistes*. To sustain and justify their interest, moreover, M. Breton had to suppose that at the heart of it all lay something which, to my mind, is clearly not there, *viz.*, some form of occult revelation.

Paul Éluard, it is true, was more affected by the verbal magic and its power to create, though presently carried away by his own rhetoric (in, we may feel, his later political direction). In 1925, he wrote of *L'Étoile au Front:*

There stand the tellers of tales. One begins, the other goes on. They are marked with the same sign, they are a prey to the same imagination which bears the earth and the heavens on its head. All the stories in the world are woven out of their words, all the world's stars are upon their brows, mysterious mirrors of the magic of dreams and of the most curious, marvellous facts. Are they likely to capture the attention of these insects who buzz faintly while eating and thinking, who barely listen to the story-tellers and certainly don't perceive the grandeur of their raving?

Prestidigitators, there they are turning pure and simple words into a crowd of personages overwhelmed by the objects of passion and what they hold in their hands is a golden ray, and what we see unfolding is truth, dignity, liberty, happiness and love.

Let Raymond Roussel show us all that never was. There are some few of us to whom that is the only reality which counts.

To-day M. Ferry, *ancien surréaliste*, is inclined to see Roussel himself as the hermetic secret. Since nobody has done more to make a public property of Roussel, it seems odd that he should write, in the issue of *Bizarre* prepared under his supervision:

Let us try to keep ourselves to ourselves. . . . Read Roussel, but don't talk about him. . . . Let us read Roussel, but not lend him out. We shouldn't get him back in good condition.

The time has come, in M. Ferry's view, to put even stouter bolts on the ivory tower.

The earliest critic to give Roussel his close attention was not a *surréaliste*, however, but that strange man, Count Robert de Montesquiou, commonly understood to be the original of Proust's Baron de Charlus and regarded as a mere freakish monster of vanity. In 1921 already, he devoted a chapter to this '*auteur difficile*' in his *Élus et Appelés*. Montesquiou states that he is acquainted with M. Roussel, but writes only of *Impressions d'Afrique* and *La Vue* and does not think it reasonable that the 'ordered nightmare' of the former should once have been put on the stage (but had not seen it and so must keep an open mind). The art of *La Vue* he describes as '*un art d'infusoire, mais, je m'empresse de l'ajouter, infusoire de génie*', an odd thing to say, though no doubt he would have conceded that genius was to be attributed rather to the microscope than to the infusoria it studied. Count Robert's essay is by no means contemptible. There was clearly more to this man than he is commonly given credit for. In describing the over-all shape of *Impressions d'Afrique*, with its parade of mysteries which are later explained, he spoke of '*équations de faits*', that is to say equations made up of facts not of figures, which then had to be solved. The expression was taken up by Roussel and is used by him, explaining his procedures, in *Comment J'Ai*. Equations of facts, in this sense, are, of course, what detective stories present us, and the detectives, with. They are also what appear notably in the opening chapters of most of the stories of Jules Verne.

Jean Cocteau's obituary notice in the *Nouvelle Revue Française* for September 1933 remains impressive.[1] The key-words are '*pureté*' and '*simplicité*'. When Cocteau describes Raymond Roussel as '*le génie à l'état pur*', that, of course, is a different sense of the word. There, '*brut*' could be substituted for '*pur*'. It is not quite the same with '*génie d'une pureté parfaite*', and Cocteau further speaks of '*cette pureté merveilleuse*' and of '*la véritable pureté*' and finally of '*l'extrême pointe de la simplicité*'. It is a quality we must all certainly recognise in Roussel's work. He was at least as much an innocent, a child of nature, as (Cocteau's own comparison) the *douanier* Rousseau in painting. A weakness in Cocteau's approach to Roussel was that it did not allow him to believe the latter when he tried to tell his new friend that he worked according to a *chiffre*, which he proposed to divulge eventually. Cocteau remained convinced that any code used must be purely instinctive, somnambulistic. The appearance of *Comment J'Ai Écrit Certains de mes Livres* two years later must have disconcerted him a little.

The purity was also hygienic, surgical, like that, says Cocteau, of his own *Enfants Terribles*, who could only live shut away in a room, unable to bear the microbes in the world outside. Like Proust, Roussel lived as though in a vacuum flask, his temperature unrelated to that elsewhere. A similar notion was expressed by Pierre Schneider in 1951 (*Cahiers du Sud*, nos. 306–7). Using the English term, he

[1] It is also still intriguing. Cocteau says that he talked with Roussel '*à la clinique de Saint-Cloud*'. This was not La Salpêtrière, and we know that Cocteau himself had a breakdown connected with opium. He describes Roussel as '*malade (et physiquement pareil à Marcel Proust)*'. In what sense like Proust physically? It may have been only some resemblance, real or imagined, in feature, build and attire, but, within the context, the suggestion rather is that their invalidism was of the same kind, so that one wonders if, at the time, Raymond Roussel also suffered from nervous asthma.

describes Roussel's world as 'dust-free'. It is also, he says, essentially a daylight world, indeed a high-noon world, in which objects cast no shadow (with the exception, we may note, of the bread-crumbs on the tablecloth upon which Spanish dancers dance in *Impressions of Africa*). M. Schneider's substantial essay is strangely headed. It is called '*La Fenêtre ou Piège à Roussel*'. It is concerned with the act of seeing among poets and with windows, optical instruments and the stage.

Both M. Schneider's essay and the Roussel chapters in the book, *Genèse de la Pensée Moderne*, published the previous year by Marcel Jean and Arpad Nezei, are further concerned with the 'abysses' in any picture of reality revealed by the fact that similar words may signify dissimilar things, that indeed identical words may signify things between which there is no element of identity whatever. The idea was made central to his argument by M. Foucault in 1963. According to M. Foucault, Roussel's adventuring among those abysses led inevitably to his suicide.

That Roussel's death took place on the actual threshold of a locked door has too much dazzled M. Foucault with its metaphorical and symbolic possibilities. M. Foucault is too fond of labyrinths, keys and thresholds, too anxious to find in Roussel's moment of death a culmination of the pattern of his work, seen too exclusively in terms of the tendency first to mystify, then to explain. All men's pre-occupations in some way 'lead to' death, since all men die. Raymond Roussel attained the age of fifty-six, which is a good deal above average for top-flight writers in our time, if we bracket off a few whose longevity was extreme. It is true that, since he was rich, he escaped pressures to which most of us are subject. It may also be true that to be rich precludes the formation of any usual sense of reality, itself at times a protection, but fifty-six is not bad for a man liable to such alternations of mood and so little a member of any community.

Nevertheless, I do not find M. Foucault's argument wholly foolish. The human world is very largely made up of words and their resonances. Most ways of life are framed within a few accepted *clichés*, and to discover that they are meaningless is as quick a road to despair as any other. Roussel's lifelong preoccupation with words that may be taken in two or more senses or which, sounding alike, point in opposed directions can hardly have failed to suggest to him that all words are treacherous and so that there *are* abysses in any picture of reality. There is a further sense in which his pairs of words in two senses may be taken as 'equations of fact', and at that point all sense of reality totters. In their blandly indifferent way, the logical positivists have directed us towards a nominalism of the same kind, but somehow contrive to preserve their own few comforting clichés intact, perhaps by concentrating mainly on the very large abstractions and believing that the concretely denotative words remain solid.

In his long-awaited and, when it came, unexpectedly short article in *Critique* for December 1963, M. Robbe-Grillet added little to the critical picture either of Roussel or of himself. He seemed, indeed, to want to dissociate himself from the master whose revival had owed a great deal to his avowal of an influence. M. Robbe-Grillet's article is called *Énigme et Transparence chez Raymond Roussel*. It is closer to Schneider than to Foucault. Each enigma is so totally explained that no element of mystery remains. The transparency results in total opacity, since there is nothing behind the transparent screen. There is a locked drawer, there is a key. The key fits the lock perfectly, and the drawer is empty. Certainly, there is no message. Raymond Roussel had nothing to say, and he said it badly. His formally constructed prose sentences lack either rhythm or harmony. You have to count on your fingers to see that each of his alexandrines contains twelve syllables.

Sight is the privileged sense in Roussel, acute to the point of madness, stretching out to the infinite and yet of things purely imaginary. Another striking characteristic of his images is their '*instantanéité*', a word we can perhaps best translate in the context as snapshot quality.

And yet it is a world from which we discover we can never get out. Everything has stopped, everything goes on reproducing itself, and the child's stick is always raised above the leaning hoop, and the spray of the motionless wave is about to fall. . . .

It is not unlike M. Robbe-Grillet's own world, perhaps more especially that of his *Instantanés*.

If that is all French criticism can offer, the outlook for a solitary Anglo-Saxon seems bleak. Luckily, I do not myself feel bound to attempt any large critical assessment. I have already set down all the information about Raymond Roussel which I thought essential. I have further completed my stint as a translator. Clearly, these two actions commit me at least to the view that Roussel is worth bothering about. It is difficult to go beyond that in a critical vacuum. I await other people's responses on both sides of the Atlantic. In the nature of things, I have to finish my work before I can form the least idea of what those responses will be. It would be a convenience if, *per impossibile*, I were able, in these last few pages, to know what I should myself then have to respond to, if, in fact, the first edition of this little book could already be a second edition.

There may be no serious critical response, but only a few more or less amiable reviews arousing no public interest whatever. Certainly, it would be folly on my part to anticipate reactions in the hope of forestalling them. If now I add a few pages in a more general vein, they should not be thought of as offering further and officious guidance but rather as taking bearings from where we are, as venturing to suggest in what context we critically stand.

It is, I suggest, primarily that of the novel or, at any rate, of narrative fiction. True, Raymond Roussel also wrote plays and verse. But, in the first place, his verse is not at present to be placed before the English-language critic and reader. His longest poem was, moreover, described by him as a novel. Though one of his two plays is, to my mind, sufficiently stageworthy, both were in large part conceived as frameworks within which stories might be told upon a stage. And it is novelists who are known to have been affected in their own practice by his work, not poets or dramatists. True, they have been novelists of the kind known also as anti-novelists. True also, neither *Impressions of Africa* nor *Locus Solus*, both to appear in translation, seems quite what is nowadays commonly understood to be a novel. Yet there is no other recognised category into which either book will fit. Both are protracted works of narrative fiction in prose. Each has characters and a story, if not much in the way of a plot. Even the fact that, especially in *Locus Solus*, the interest is concentrated rather on self-contained stories within the general narrative framework than on the general narrative itself does not remove these books from the context of the novel as it was at one time understood.

It must nevertheless be conceded that the sort of Anglo-American criticism most highly regarded at present and likeliest to find a profitable subject in Roussel has concerned itself rather with poets than with novelists, with James Joyce, certainly, but perhaps more conspicuously with Yeats, Blake and Eliot. I mean, of course, that vocabulary-computing, image-busting criticism practised most insistently in American but latterly more and more in at least some British universities. To high-powered academic practitioners in that field, what has been done with the four writers listed above would seem child's play to what might be attempted with Raymond Roussel, if only their type of criticism could once be brought to bear upon him. Unfortunately, he is not yet established as a subject among us, and he made the mistake of writing in French. For that sort of criticism does not yet seem much to thrive in the French departments of universities on either side of the Atlantic, despite a few brilliant bi-lingualists like Mr. Bruce Morrissette, to whom I can think off-hand of no British equivalent.

I shall, therefore, if I may, nag a little at that idea of the novel to which everybody subscribes in his off-moments. I do not in the least wish to deny that there has been a 'great age of the novel' in that sense. I will dote with the next man on Jane Austen, Balzac, 'George Eliot', Stendhal, Flaubert, Dickens, the great Russians, Hardy, Conrad and D. H. Lawrence, drawing the line a little at William

Faulkner and regarding not only Joyce but also Proust and even Benjamin Constant as anti-novelists, as indeed was Jane Austen in her earlier books. There was a great age of capitalism, and it coincided with a great age of the novel.

The philosopher of the great age of capitalism was Hegel, with Marx as the follower who stood both dialectic and synthesis on their heads, a sorcerer's apprentice who made everything worse by a misappropriation of the spells which nobody has yet found a way of putting right. The idea was that forms evolve towards a state of perfection. There is a quasi-Hegelian or post-Hegelian idea of the novel, as there is of the necessary course of social and political development. In literary history, the notion broadly is that the true novel or novel proper always existed as a latent idea in the minds of men and that once or twice, sporadically, it seemed about to emerge in earlier times, in ancient Rome, for instance, and in medieval Japan, that it stirred powerfully again in Spain in the sixteenth century, then, later and even more powerfully, in France, and that here, after a hundred years of vigorous false starts, it finally bloomed with Jane Austen and Sir Walter Scott, since when in essence the form has remained unchanging. Occasionally, some nation which has not previously gone in for novel-writing may bring its national genius to the enlargement, which is at the same time a consolidation, of the idea, the two most notable cases to date being that of the Russians in the nineteenth century and the Americans more recently, so that the great American novel is still to write.

I do not myself subscribe to this evolutionary optimism, either politically or aesthetically. I do not believe in the classless society or the world-state, and I am sure we should not like them if we had them. Things change, but not necessarily for the better. Marvellous things were done in the name of progress, but progressivism gone rotten is now a pervasive nuisance. For a hundred years, great things were written by persons who subscribed to the idea of a novel proper or true novel, but the idea now simply fills publishers' lists with rubbish and bedevils the work of writers who might be doing something more amusing.

To me, it is part of the charm of Raymond Roussel that his writings are totally devoid of seriousness. They may obscurely search the reader's heart, but they do not set out to reveal the truth about that troublesome and unreliable organ, let alone to explore the position of man in society, any more than do the farces of P. G. Wodehouse or the ingenious contrivances of a writer of good detective stories. These are not, indeed, though structurally identical, regarded as true novels or novels proper. The increasingly irksome characteristic of true novels or novels proper is their seriousness, their *trompe l'oeil* verisimilitude, their apparent preoccupation with human reality and truth, although everyone knows that a novel is in the first place a pack of lies, however much 'imaginative truth' it may be held in the last place to contain.

A term which has only quite recently come into general critical use, in English, is 'novella', recognised by its users as an Italian word and sometimes given its correct Italian plural form as 'novelle'. It is used to mean what not long ago was known as a 'long-short' story, it being well understood in those days that the French term was 'nouvelle', itself sometimes used as the Italian term is now. No doubt, both then and now, it was and is further borne in mind that our word 'novel' shares a common origin with those French and Italian terms. The natural perversity of foreigners may have been held to account for the fact that the French and the Italians themselves somehow came to use different words for what we regard as novels, the French using 'roman' and the Italians 'romanzo', terms related to our 'romance'. For the sake of completeness, it may further be noted that to Spaniards a novel, as we understand it, is still a *novela*, while to Germans it may be either a *Novelle* or a *Roman*, German ears and eyes having been for so long directed outside their own country, while, in a literary historian's purview, the Spaniards may be considered to have invented the novel, as they invented capitalistic imperialism, and then to have let both go.

The Oxford dictionaries commit themselves to the view that the Italian feminine singular 'novella' represents a Latin neuter plural identical with it in form, so that it first meant 'news'. This itself is a rather odd plural formation. It is used singularly in English. We say that the news is bad, not that they are bad. This is not the case in French or Spanish, where the feminine plurals, '*nouvelles*' and '*nuevas*', are so treated grammatically. German allows a variety of singular and plural forms, not all connected with the idea of novelty. Italian still allows '*novella*' and two other feminine singulars.

That the novel is the merest novelty, as transient as yesterday's newspaper, is a notion which has never quite been dispelled and which review columns in the weeklies and publishers' account books largely confirm. But, indeed, neither have the terms '*romanzo*', '*roman*' and 'romance' escaped an obloquy varying in tone, meaning and intensity according to time, place and social ambience. The idea of a novel as the merest novelty was strong all through the eighteenth century, when the idea of the 'great' novel (a product later thought to be as durable as epic verse) had not yet been formed and when (with *The Spectator* and others) there were indeed great newspapers, which have outlived most of the novels of their day. Late in the century, Diderot, because of the greater 'realism' of English novels, expressed the wish that a term other than '*roman*' could be found for them in French. That was the moment at which, in English, the idea of a novel proper or true novel first began to emerge. Yet the term '*roman*' has persisted in French for works of far more conspicuous realism than those of Samuel Richardson.

During the past ten years, much has been heard of the anti-novel. The term '*anti-roman*' was put into its present circulation by Jean-Paul Sartre in 1947 to describe the first novel of Nathalie Sarraute. The term had, however, been used three hundred and twenty years before, when Charles Sorel published *Le Berger Extravagant, ou l'Anti-Roman*. It could, indeed, be argued that, in significant literary history, the anti-novel preceded the novel. The earliest 'novel' any large number of people still think worth reading is *Don Quixote*, a parody of the romances of its time, an anti-novel in the sense intended by the Sieur de Souvigny.

Between the dates of first publication of *Don Quixote* and *Le Berger Extravagant*, there appeared in London a first and very fine anonymous English translation of the *Decameron*, a book which bears some resemblance to Raymond Roussel's works in prose, in that it groups occasions for story-telling within a framework elaborately conceived. Clearly, the divergence of 'novel' from *'novella'* had not taken place by 1620. The ladies and gentlemen being installed at their villa outside Florence, Pampinea says:

You see, fair company, that the sun is highly mounted and the heat elsewhere too extreme for us, and therefore here is our fittest refuge, the air being so cool and delicate. Here are tables, cards and chess as your dispositions may be addicted, but if mine advice might pass for current, I would admit none of those exercises because they are too troublesome both to them that play and such as look on. I could rather wish that some quaint discourse might pass among us, a tale or fable related by some one to urge the attention of all the rest, and so, wearing out the warmth of the day, one pretty novel will draw on another until the sun be lower declined and the heat's extremity more diminished.

I suppose that most of Boccaccio's inserted stories would qualify to-day as *novelle*, though not all are long-short. The crane's leg story, told on the sixth day by Neiphila, is decidedly short-short. The story from which Keats took *The Pot of Basil* (Philomena's on the fourth day) is on the short side, and even the greatly admired tale of Frederigo's falcon (told on the fifth day by Fiammetta) is not above magazine length. None of all the hundred pretty novels would be regarded as a novel today. We, on the other hand, do not regard the whole work as a novel.

Perhaps we should. The framework description of the plague in Florence is as fine as any of the stories themselves, and this is ordinarily forgotten when Boccaccio is written about by critics. I, certainly, should be happy to leave Raymond Roussel in, as we might say, a Boccaccio context, making, however, one additional point about the state of narrative fiction today. In Boccaccio, there is no underpinning of the superficial narrative by myth or whatever.

James Joyce's *Ulysses* started a trend in this respect in 1922, that *annus mirabilis* which might well be set as a term to the history of the true novel or novel proper. Earlier, Greek epic had provided an underpinning to the great novels of that very great man, Henry Fielding. In recent years, Vladimir Nabokov's *Pale Fire* delighted us all with a novel elaborately underpinned. I do not at all wish to belittle Nabokov when I say that I see him as much influenced by Raymond Queneau, whose first novel, *Le Chiendent*, explicitly influenced by Joyce, was, in 1933, most elaborately underpinned, as, twenty years later, was M. Robbe-Grillet's first novel, *Les Gommes*, with the Oedipus myth and the *arcana* of the Tarot pack.

M. Queneau in those days a close friend of Michel Leiris, must certainly have been acquainted with Roussel's work. M. Robbe-Grillet, we know, certainly was. I cannot answer for Mr. Nabokov. I cannot answer for Señor Jorge Luis Borges, whose marvellous *Fictions* seem to me to have much in common with Roussel, but who is blind and can deal with letters only through an intermediary.

APPENDIX

THE GREENISH SKIN

La peau verdâtre de la prune un peu mûre. . . . The greenish skin of the ripening plum looked as appetising as anybody could wish. I therefore chose this fruit among the various delicacies made ready on a silver platter against the *señora's* return.

With the point of a knife I made a tiny hole in the delicate peel, and, taking a phial from my pocket, I poured in several drops of a rapid poison.

'You betrayed me, Natte,' I said in a toneless voice. 'Now let fate conclude!'

And I returned the mortal fruit to its place.

I was stifling beneath my *picador's* costume, my wig and my big hat. The chandeliers in the drawing-room rivalled in brilliance the footlight reflectors, by which I was dazzled. Black garments hung upon all the doors, and the rows of gilded chairs were everywhere strewn with spangled, low-necked, white evening gowns. No detail was missing in this Spanish great lady's room. Jingling harness and the crack of a whip, suddenly heard off-stage, told me Natte had returned.

I quickly seized my voluminous black cape, thrown over a chair as I came in, and sprang upon the bed, between whose closely drawn curtains I was able to see without being seen.

Natte appeared. This was the lady of the house in person, still beautiful at the age of forty-six, thanks to the care she lavished upon her person. By some means known only to herself, her complexion in particular was miraculously preserved, and her hair was of an intense and dazzling black. Her features had unfortunately not quite escaped the ravages of time. Make-up did not wholly conceal a number of wrinkles at the corners of her eyes and mouth.

Little Madame Dé, charming in the costume of an Andalusian maidservant, had also entered. Dismissed by Natte after a brief exchange, she departed with her mistress's cloak. Left alone, Natte sat down to her supper.

'Turquoise, o Turquoise, my beloved!' she cried out, her voice a-quiver.

Turquoise was a young muleteer with whom Natte was deceiving me. An intercepted letter, telling me all, had impelled me to the fell deed.

'The thought of you is sweet, Turquoise, o Turquoise, my young lover!' said Natte again, her gaze dreamingly astray.

Then, rising, all agitation:

'Lord God! If Mirliton knew, he would kill me!...'

I was Mirliton, the abandoned *picador*. Dismissing her cares, Natte sat down again to eat. She was the Spanish type to perfection, with the two beauty spots, one on her cheek, one on her chin, and her marvellous black hair, which reflected the stage lighting, obliterated all thought of her ravaged features.

'What is Turquoise doing at this moment?' she murmured, between a piece of sandwich cake and a little tart. 'He is thinking of me, as I of him.'

From my observation post, I attentively watched her supper diminish. Natte endeavoured to calm her agitation.

'Mirliton can know nothing; he loves me, trusts me....'

She had just finished an apricot; only the fatal fruit remained on the platter. She took it between two fingers.

'If Mirliton yet knew,' she continued, her voice deep.

Then she bit....

The effect was instantaneous. She rose to open a window, as if suffocating, turned about several times beating the air with her arms and fell dead upon the carpet.

I reached the floor in one bound and ran to put out the candles burning in two silver candlesticks on the table. At once all the lights went out, both the drawing-room chandeliers and the footlights. Alone, a broad ray of moonlight shone, through the open window, upon the corpse.

I took my cape off the bed, the great black cape in which I was accustomed to envelop myself, and spread it wide over Natte's body. Then I knelt beside her in silence.

Motionless, Natte seemed marble. The black cape covered her entirely. Only the head was visible, its black hair gleaming, the aging face pallid beneath shifting moonlight which poured, almost green, from the window.

The effect was tragic.

One thing only was visible, only one. . . .

The greenish skin of the dark Spanish beauty, no longer young. . . .
La peau verdâtre de la brune un peu mûre.